THE
RICHEST
MAN IN TOWN

THE
RICHEST
MAN IN TOWN

The TWELVE
COMMANDMENTS
of WEALTH

W. RANDALL JONES

BUSINESS
PLUS

NEW YORK   BOSTON

Business Plus
Hachette Book Group
237 Park Avenue
New York, NY 10017
Visit our Web site at www.HachetteBookGroup.com.

Business Plus is an imprint of Grand Central Publishing.
The Business Plus name and logo are trademarks of Hachette Book Group, Inc.

Printed in the United States of America

First Edition: May 2009

10 9 8 7 6 5 4 3 2

Library of Congress Cataloging-in-Publication Data

Jones, W. Randall.
   The richest man in town: the twelve commandments of wealth /
W. Randall Jones. — 1st ed.
      p. cm.
   Includes index.
   Summary: "A definitive exploration as well as prescriptive advice of the key common traits of the wealthiest people who live in your town." —Provided by the publisher.
   ISBN 978-0-446-53783-4
1. Success in business—United States. 2. Wealth—United States. 3. Millionaires—United States. I. Title.
   HF5386.J784 2009
   332.024'01—dc22

                                                        2008044111

Book design by Charles Sutherland

For Dad, who made us all feel like the richest man in town

CONTENTS

AUTHOR'S NOTE

As I grew up among the tall pines of Carrollton, Georgia—a town of twenty thousand of the nicest people on earth, most of whom had never been to New York—I never dreamed of one day living in the big city, or running with the big dogs (that's what we call the rich and famous in my hometown). I did dream, however, of being a writer. Thirty years later, I can say that I have lived in the big city, and as this book attests I have been blessed to run with the "big dogs." It is my sincere hope that after twenty-five years in magazine publishing with *Esquire*, *Civilization*, *The American Benefactor*, and *Worth*, a book titled *The Greatest Stock Picks of All Time*, and now with this labor of love, I have proven myself as a writer. But of course, I will let you be the judge of that.

Back in the 1960s, in the hamlet of Carrollton, I lived in a nice house at the top of the hill, overlooking acres and acres of Jones land that had been in my family for generations. As idyllic as the view was then, and is still today, I often found myself dreaming of a different view and a different life. Not necessarily a better life, but rather a richer life, in the most meaningful and existential sense of the word *rich*. To see the grandeur and glories of the world, to know the most interesting people around the globe, and to experience, learn, and truly understand the best that this wonderful world has to offer: Those were my dreams.

Quite simply, I wanted to succeed. Admittedly, I was not exactly sure what success really meant. I dreamed of living in a sizable home with two-story columns—I have. I dreamed of making a seven-figure salary—I have. More important, I dreamed of a life of constant learning. Thankfully, I'm still very much in the process. And yes, I secretly dreamed of being rich, yet I was not at all certain what that really meant. I've done well, but full disclosure: I am not the richest man in town—certainly not in New York City, or in Carrollton, Georgia, the two towns that I call home today. I am not done yet, however, and I trust neither are you.

My curiosity is perhaps the character trait of which I am most proud. The most successful people I have known along my journey to this richer and fuller life share this one critical character trait—boundless, near-insatiable curiosity. Samuel Johnson, the most quoted English writer other than Shakespeare, had it right when he said, "Curiosity is, in great and generous minds, the first passion and the last." It is mine.

In conceiving this book, I found I was most curious about people, because from others, I believe we learn our most vital and valuable lessons in life. Second only to our own mistakes and unique experiences, we learn best from the experiences of those whom we most admire and respect—and in rare cases those we detest. I am and have always been most interested in and intrigued by those men and women who by dint of their own talent, ingenuity, creativity, promise, and perseverance accomplish truly great things and amass great wealth as a well-deserved byproduct of their accomplishments.

This book is replete with such people. It is a treasure trove of their personal experiences, their triumphs, their failures, and—most important—their wisdom. It is not your run-of-the-mill get-rich book. It is not one man's or one woman's story. It is instead the collective wisdom and proven wealth-creation philosophies of one hundred of America's greatest success stories. All of them self-made—actually, the term I prefer is one Birmingham, Alabama's richest man in town, Miller Gorrie, coined: *self-*

sufficient—successes. Yes, they have all attained a staggering amount of wealth, but, much more significant, most have attained a monumental degree of satisfaction in their lives by contributing real value to the world. They have not led the "life of quiet desperation" that nineteenth-century philosopher Henry David Thoreau so feared. They are hunters and explorers, constantly seeking new ideas, new ways of thinking, and new opportunities. They both love and value the thrill of each quest. Their expeditions excite them, fuel their passions, and, not surprisingly, make them truly happy. They are living the American Dream.

THE
RICHEST
MAN IN TOWN

PART I

IT'S GOOD TO BE RICH

MY AMERICAN DREAM

Secretly, if not overtly, almost everyone in America desires to become rich: to make it big and enjoy the fruits of a prosperous life. So if the desire is there, why do the vast majority of Americans never achieve great success and its attendant rewards? Simply put, most of us do not have a clue about how to reach this all-too-elusive position. We have no proven blueprint for reaching greatness, no cleverly devised plan, and almost certainly little or no access to those who have actually accomplished the feat of becoming the richest person in town. It is my American Dream that this book will give every young man or woman with an ounce of ambition a personal road map and the inspiration to embark on the journey. Furthermore, I hope that *The Richest Man in Town* will also reach out and grab those who are adrift, those who have experienced failure or temporary setbacks, or those who haven't yet found their path to success. Whether you are eighteen or fifty-eight, the lessons I have learned from the most successful Americans will, I hope, inspire, cajole, and mentor you to that rich, full, and successful life of which you have dreamed and I hope you deserve.

A Word About the Word *Rich*

I admit it. I love the word *rich*, but not in the pejorative "filthy lucre" meaning of the word. As I was growing up in the South, *rich* was often thought of as a four-letter word, a term not used in polite company. One simply did not discuss religion, politics, sex, or money—all my favorite subjects. Not surprisingly, today I see things differently. Now I think of this powerful adjective in its most holistic sense. When I think *rich*, I think of a life of bountiful joy, of sincere goodness, filled with great worth and value. I think of things that are magnificent, sumptuous, beautiful, and of people being rich in ideas, spirit, and generosity. I think of abundance, of fertile land, of meaningful, significant, productive lives, and, yes, of profitable enterprises—I think of rich as being financially sound and secure.

Legendary billionaire oil baron J. Paul Getty, once the richest man in the world, said, "Richness is at least as much about character, philosophy, outlook and attitude as it is about money." So true. How wise. Money may be the scorecard, the easiest barometer of success to measure, but it is only one component of the American Dream.

When I was launching *Worth* magazine in the early 1990s, I said to anyone willing to listen, "Money is simply a means to an end—that end being a richer, fuller, more exciting and dynamic life." My belief was then and continues to be today that money in and of itself is not evil, but rather gains its meaning from the ways in which it is earned and the ways in which it is utilized. Most successful and secure people agree. The subjects of this book certainly do. They also agree that a mother lode of money without personal fulfillment is bona fide failure, pure psychic bankruptcy. Believe me, the richest men and women in town are constantly in search of true fulfillment, not just financial riches. The riches flow from the fulfillment of their passions, from the contributions of value they make, and from the successes of their enterprises. Their quests to fulfillment are the basis of this book. The common elements of their personal success expeditions show us the way we each can become the richest person in town if and only if we heed their collective advice.

Every Town Has One

A richest man or woman, that is. Without serious thought or reading farther, you probably have an idea who is the most successful person in your hometown. Often this is the largest employer, the most generous philanthropist, the most admired; very often, it's the most colorful or even the most feared person in town. One thing is certain—this person holds considerable sway over their town; his or her influence is unquestioned. So who is the richest self-sufficient person in New York, Los Angeles, Sacramento, or Savannah? *The Richest Man in Town* isolates these folks in a hundred American towns, delving into their psyches to reveal their very personal stories and, more important, their wisdom on wealth creation. They have all achieved their own American Dream; now, many of them for the first time have taken time to reflect on how they did it, what they learned along the way, and what advice they would give to their best friend or their own children or grandchildren.

It was my intention that *The Richest Man in Town* would be the most substantive and substantial collective analysis of modern America's most successful self-made individuals to date. It is also perhaps the only analysis of the proven ways in which one gets mega-rich in America today. F. Scott Fitzgerald may have been right when he wrote, "The rich are different from you and me." Of course, they have more money, way more money, but are they really that different? What sets them apart, other than copious amounts of cash? What are the commonalities among these hundred self-sufficient individuals? Did they set out to get rich, or did their success evolve over time? What is the one thing that most affected their success? Who was their role model or mentor—if they even had one? What is the true secret or secrets to their success? Are they religious? What role has marriage or partnership played in their success? At what age did they make it big? Who do they most admire? What were the most important steps they took to achieve such monumental success? What were the hardest lessons they learned in their journey to becoming the richest person in town?

It's Good to Be Rich

For the record, I believe strongly that it is good to be rich and that the self-made rich (most of them, anyway) are, at heart, good people. A few years ago, I spearheaded a special anniversary edition of *Worth* magazine called The Richest Person in Town. In the issue, we surveyed the hundred largest towns in America by population, uncovering the richest person in each. Our goal was to paint a truly representative portrait of wealth in America. Too often, we view wealth and success through the lenses of New York and Hollywood. As important as these two engines of commerce and creativity are, they are not representative of success in this huge and diverse country of three hundred million people. America is vast; success and wealth reside all across this great nation. As interesting as the original *Worth* list was, in truth, we didn't analyze the commonalities among these extraordinary individuals, nor did we distinguish between self-made wealth and inherited riches. *The Richest Man in Town* changes all that. I have scoured hundreds of American towns to uncover the most compelling and prescriptive success stories of our time. In my journey, I was struck by so many people who were living the American Dream that one of the greatest challenges was simply deciding which ones to interview.

In the end, all fifty states are represented in this survey, proving that the American Dream is not only alive and well but clearly attainable in any town, anywhere in America. My goal was simple: to determine the state of self-sufficient success and wealth creation in America today, but also, more important, to shed light on the ways in which we can learn from the triumphs and the trials of these fabled folks. Notice I said rich and successful; I did not mention the word *famous*. Though some of these successes are indeed famous, most are not. They are not national household names by any measure, though they are quite well known by many, if not most, in the towns they call home.

Why the *Richest Man in Town* Title?

Because ninety-six of the hundred most financially successful self-made people in the chosen hundred towns are, well, men. I realize this book does not prove that women have shattered the so-called glass ceiling, certainly not the glass ceiling of wealth creation, but I found powerful evidence that many women are gaining fast on these local icons. My editor, Rick Wolff, also believes that the title *Richest Man in Town* simply has a more lyrical, familiar ring than the more accurate *Richest Person in Town*. For me, the inspiration came from one of America's (and my) favorite movies of all time, *It's a Wonderful Life*, in which Jimmy Stewart as George Bailey so positively affected the lives of his fellow citizens in fictional Bedford Falls that his brother raises a toast to him at the end of the movie saying, "To George Bailey—the richest man in town." Because Stewart's George Bailey saved the town and many of the townspeople from financial ruin due to a greedy slumlord and a run on the bank (sound familiar?), he deserved the title in the richest sense of the compliment. Also, our literary and contemporary culture has produced these American archetypes, from Jay Gatsby to Citizen Kane; from Don Corleone to the *Simpsons* character Montgomery Burns. Or maybe it's just that we all know, or at least conjecture constantly, about who is "the richest man" in our own hometowns.

The Rich Research

I spent more than two years interviewing local business editors and community leaders in a hundred towns across America to uncover the most successful and, yes, the richest self-made persons in each. The friends I have met during my career of covering the wealthy were my most valuable resource and source of introductions. Subsequently, I used all available public data, including Hoover's, LexisNexis, SEC filings, *Forbes*, EDGAR, and The Rich List, to value their public holdings. I even "Zillowed" their residences for valuations. I interviewed local newspaper editors, bankers, and investment bankers in an attempt to value privately held companies, but in the end I was not terribly interested in the exact amount of wealth they had accumulated. What I was after was the ways in which they created their own unique success.

All net worth estimates are therefore just that—informed hypotheses. It is impossible to calculate the net worth of folks who have achieved this kind of remarkable financial success with complete accuracy. And given what has transpired in this most recent economic crisis, it would be foolhardy. In the final analysis, though, it is just as J. Paul Getty, the billionaire oil tycoon, once said, "If you can actually count your money, you are not really a rich man."

Nevertheless, my research indicates that the poorest of these richest folks in town (hereafter referred to as RMITs or RWITs) is conservatively worth in excess of $100 million. For most ambitious Americans, that amount will probably suffice. Getty also observed that, "Money is like manure. You have to spread it around or it smells." I would add that wisdom follows the same rule. Sharing this wisdom is why I have gathered the stories, advice, and cumulative intelligence of these truly extraordinary individuals who have achieved success, in most cases, beyond their wildest dreams.

The You Factor

The ultimate question is, of course, how does all of this apply to you? It doesn't, unless you're ready to change a few things in your life. It alters nothing unless you're prepared to open your mind to the possibilities, to believe that with diligence, desire, and some proven, smart direction that you, too, can become one of the most successful people in America. If you have not yet achieved the American Dream, you must be willing to change. Billy Joe "Red" McCombs, San Antonio's most successful serial entrepreneur and without doubt its most colorful character, says, "You've got to be willing to change what you are doing and the way you have been doing things or you will continue to produce the same old results."

Charles Darwin was thus right, I believe, when he observed: "It is not the strongest of the species that survive, nor the most intelligent, but the ones most responsive to change." It's never too late to change your life, but you have to be willing to make the effort. "When you're through changing, you're simply through," notes McCombs. He should know. He was a millionaire (when a million bucks was real money) before his thirtieth birthday. More than fifty years ago, he began building his fortune by selling cars; he owned his first dealership by the age of twenty-five. Ultimately, he became the sixth largest automobile dealer in the United States. McCombs is the co-founder, with fellow San Antonio bigwig Lowry Mays, of Clear Channel, the media and entertainment conglomerate, which is the largest owner of radio stations in the United States. He is a major real estate developer who once owned the San Antonio Spurs, the Denver Nuggets, and the Minnesota Vikings. According to the *San Antonio Business Journal*, he bought the Vikings for less than $250 million and sold them for $625 million. McCombs knows how to make a profit, and he knows the power of change.

How Much Is Richest-Man-in-Town Rich?

What is rich anyway? What does that really mean? How much money does it take to be rich in modern America? The eminent satirist and journalist H. L. Mencken once defined a wealthy man as "one who earns $100 a year more than his wife's sister's husband." Understandably, then, *rich* is a very personal term and a highly individual amount.

The average RMIT has a net worth of more than $3.5 billion. Fifty of the one hundred on the list are currently billionaires. The total wealth of America's RMITs is a stunning $355 billion, which represents 7.4 percent of America's total wealth of approximately $48 trillion. The poorest RMIT is $100 million rich and the richest is Bill Gates—worth more than $50 billion, the second richest man in America, behind Warren Buffett. (Note: I did not choose Warren Buffett as the RMIT of Omaha, Nebraska, because so much has already been written about him. In truth, I was more interested in Buffett's neighbor, Joe Ricketts, the quiet billionaire who created what is today TD Ameritrade.) Stunningly, while America's RMITs control better than 7 percent of the nation's wealth, the top 1 percent of the demographic pyramid currently controls almost 35 percent of the total wealth. The top 10 percent controls an astounding 70 percent of the nation's wealth. The concentration of riches has never been, well, more concentrated. According to the Federal Reserve, there are approximately nine million millionaires in the United States and 517,000 deca-millionaires (worth $10 million or more).

Phil Ruffin, the RMIT of Wichita, Kansas, offers a common RMIT sentiment: "Liquid assets, however, are the truest test of what is really rich—stocks, bonds, and cash." He should know. On the day I interviewed him, he was buying a billion dollars' worth of bonds on the heels of having sold thirty-four acres of land on the Las Vegas Strip for a record $1.4 billion. Unlike

RMITs, many Americans might appear outwardly rich—what my Texas friends call "all hat and no cattle." They have all the trappings—the big house, the fine cars, the shimmering jewels—but if they had to put their hands on $15 million of ransom money in twenty-four hours, they would be hard-pressed. Ruffin says, "There are a lot of people who have a couple of billion in assets, but when you see that cash in the bank every morning, then you know you're really rich."

One thing all RMITs have in common is that they have plenty of cattle, figuratively speaking—they are liquid-asset-rich. The other is that they have created their success and amassed their fortunes without the help of inheritance. They are all self-made. Let's be clear about the definition of *self-made*, though. I don't believe that anyone is ever entirely self-made, not those of us living in the democracy of America anyway. With public schools, scholarship opportunities, and financial aid, almost anyone can get a great education in America—that provides a head start. With tax incentives and governmental research that benefits private enterprise, we all are equal inheritors of these democratic gifts. Without question, coming from a more privileged educational or societal background can give a significant advantage, but no degree of head start can buy the traits and beliefs of the most successful Americans—the richest people in town.

Statistics suggest then that being self-sufficiently rich means having a net worth of $10 million or more. Most of us can live quite lavishly on $10 million. Is $10 million or more within your grasp? This book proves it is most certainly possible. Remember, the poorest RMIT (poor soul) is worth an estimated $100 million. That amount of money then is ten times what it takes to be really rich by modern standards. The good news is that this is within your grasp. It's time to grab hold of the American Dream.

THE AMERICAN DREAM: UP CLOSE AND PERSONAL

What is the American Dream? When asked to define the American Dream, RMITs cite freedom as the greatest by-product of their success—other than the money, of course. Freedom to live as they please, freedom to be a perpetual student, freedom to use philanthropy as a mechanism to change the world, or simply freedom to do just about anything their innate, unique abilities allow them to achieve. Cynics like the late comedian George Carlin have said, "The reason they call it the American Dream is because you have to be asleep to believe it." RMITs really don't buy into that kind of cynicism (and by the way, George Carlin also died a very rich man). RMITs appreciate the humor, but they feel strongly that $100 million or more does, indeed, buy a lot of freedom and a lot of happiness.

Jorge (he prefers the pronunciation of *George*) Pérez is the richest man in Miami, Florida. The real estate mogul of Related Industries and the most successful Hispanic American in the United States, he has his mark on virtually every condominium building with blue-water views of the Atlantic Ocean. "The American Dream is the freedom to do the things you want to do with the people you want to do them with," he says. "That's success." He should know. He fought hard to get here from Argentina and Colombia as the son of Cuban exiles.

Peter Nicholas, the co-founder of Boston Scientific, notes that those who are cynical about financial success usually do not have the drive or the ability to achieve the American Dream. He warns, "There's a big difference between long-term sustainable success and fast bubble success." The whiplash of the last Internet bubble is indelibly etched in his mind, as are the dizzying recent market gyrations. David Jones of Humana fame, Louisville, Kentucky's top slugger and definitely a long-term success, says, "You're living the American Dream if your children are independent. It's also great if you have created jobs for your community. I figure I have created over a hundred thousand jobs with my businesses."

Robert Jepson Jr., Savannah, Georgia's savant of success, says the American Dream is "having the greatest number of personal options to do good in one's life: to provide for others, to live a productive life, to be able to provide for one's community, and to be recognized by your peers as successful in your personal endeavors." He admits, though, that since he made his fortune in the buying and selling of companies, much of his definition of the American Dream is now in the accumulation of wealth. With major successes in the three businesses that he has built or turned around (more on that later), Jepson has spent his well-earned wealth at least partially on a great lifestyle and in his powerful philanthropic works. Perhaps his proudest achievement, though, is endowing the Jepson School of Leadership Studies at his alma mater, the University of Richmond.

When I asked the RMIT in Dayton, Ohio, Clayton Mathile (pronounced *ma-TEEL*), how he personally defined the American Dream, he said, without any hesitation, "Applause at home." He says this means your wife loves you, your kids love you, and your best friends love you. Sometimes the simple truths are, indeed, the most powerful. Even though Mathile has billions in the bank thanks to his success with Iams, the premium pet foods company that he sold to Procter and Gamble in 1999 for $2.3 billion, he still reverts to what he considers true success—the love and respect of family and friends. He says, "I didn't want to look back on my life and think that my biggest accomplishment was just making a big ol' pile of money." The former farm boy did have a hard time selling the company that had come to define him, however. He says his wife, Mary, used to joke that Iams was "like their sixth child who grew up, but wouldn't leave home." That sixth child did finally leave home in what was at that time the largest acquisition P&G had ever made.

Clay Mathile agrees with Ralph Waldo Emerson, who said, "To laugh often and much; To win the respect of intelligent people and the affection of children; To earn the appreciation of honest critics and endure the betrayal of false friends; To appreciate beauty, to find the best in others: To leave the world a bit better, whether by a healthy child, a garden patch, or a redeemed social condition; To know even one life has breathed easier because you have lived. This is to have succeeded." Perhaps this is why Mathile has built a 114-acre campus just outside Dayton called the Center for Entrepreneurial Education where he spends much of his time today in a post-pet-foods world. He wants to use his considerable resources and expertise giving local entrepreneurs the education and mentoring to one day enjoy a self-made success similar to his. These are the kinds of rewards that RMITs seem to enjoy most. These are their American Dreams.

What About the Odds?

How likely are you to become an RMIT? If, as we know, there are more than nine million millionaires in this land of three hundred million Americans, that means approximately one in every thirty-three thousand of us is a millionaire. You also now know of the fallacy that the rich in America are all a part of the Lucky Sperm Club. Fully 90 percent of all wealth in America today is first-generation wealth. There is not a Rockefeller, Vanderbilt, or Whitney written about in this collection of RMITs. The folks in this book are all self-made. Further, two-thirds of the current Forbes 400 list (the four hundred richest people in the country) are also self-made, proving once again that America is still the land of opportunity where anyone can make it, if you have the right stuff or choose to cultivate the right stuff.

Money and Time

There is one element that $100 million or more of net worth can't buy—time. The very rich are no different from anyone else when it comes to this highly prized commodity. We all have the same twenty-four hours in each day. As is noted in the Broadway musical *Rent*, there are 525,600 minutes in a year. But it's not how many minutes there are, it's what we do with those minutes that matters, and in many ways this determines whether you will become the most successful person in your hometown. Biotech billionaire Randal J. "RJ" Kirk of Belspring, Virginia, a town that consists mostly of his six-thousand-acre farm with its own runway for landing his private jet, says, "The only relationship we have to the future is through this moment in time." He adds, "This architecture of thinking emphasizes the importance of optimizing now. This moment in time is all we have, so we must make the most it."

It is readily apparent to me that RMITs optimize their time better than most of us. This key ability is one of the principal reasons for their blazing success and hefty bank accounts. RMITs also appear to need much less sleep than the rest of us. Former air force pilot and real estate developer Leroy Landhuis of Colorado Springs says, "I have a physiological phenomenon that requires me to need almost no sleep. I don't sleep more than twelve to fifteen hours a week max, but I function at the same level whether I sleep or not. Consequently I get a lot more opportunity to read."

Almost embarrassed, Providence, Rhode Island's Jonathan Nelson, the private equity prince whose firm Providence Equity Partners recently completed the largest leveraged buyout in history (in excess of $50 billion) and who owns movie studio MGM, explains his work ethic by quoting Shakespeare's powerful refrain: "The test of a vocation is the love of its drudgery." He says, "I don't sleep much. I work way too much, but it's because I truly enjoy it." Peter Drucker, a management expert and philosopher hero to many RMITs, was famous for saying, "There are not 24 hours in a day—there are only two to three that matter. It's what you do with those two to three hours that determines one's success." Savannah's Bob Jepson agrees: "Time is the greatest gift we have and I don't want to waste a minute of it. I want to get up every day and have it include some joy, some happiness, not only for me, but everybody around me." San Antonio's Red McCombs sums it up this way: "Time is a million times more valuable than money—you can always get more money, but you cannot get more time."

What follows are American RMITs' very personal stories and the Twelve Commandments to finding and enjoying success and wealth in America today. Unlike the thousands of diet books that come and go on the market—each promising a better way to lose weight and stay fit with its own unique gimmick—*The Richest Man in Town* has no get-rich-quick gimmicks, just the proven methods of the most successful self-made people of our time. As Bernard Marcus, the richest self-made man in Atlanta and the founder of Home Depot, told me, "It takes a long time and a lot of hard work to become an overnight success. It took me twenty-five years." David Green, the Oklahoma City success story and founder of Hobby Lobby who says he doesn't consider himself self-made—he prefers the term *God-made*—

concurred with Marcus when he said, "I have worked thirty years to become an instant success." Here's wishing you great joy on your passage to becoming the richest man or woman in town. Remember, these RMITs prove that the joy is in the journey.

WHO ARE AMERICA'S RMITs?

Business legend has it that there are three types of people: those who make things happen, those who watch things happen, and those who have no idea what is happening. American RMITs, not surprisingly, are those who make things happen. They make big things happen. They thrill in ideation and even more in execution. Quite simply, they are builders—they love to create and build more than anything else. They build businesses, they build homes, and they build great wealth.

The vast majority of them say they are ultra-happy as well, and they all agree on one thing—retirement sucks! With a conservative net worth of $6 billion, Sam Zell is the richest man in Chicago. He's a real estate titan and recent buyer of the Tribune Company, the media colossus that encompasses the *Chicago Tribune*, the *Los Angeles Times*, and the *Baltimore Sun*. When I asked him, "What's next?" he replied, "Who knows? I just know there will be something and it will be fascinating—I'm a professional opportunist." What follows is the collective wisdom of one hundred "professional opportunists" who uniquely define the American Dream.

America's RMITs—The Greatest Success Stories of Our Time

Akron, OH: James Oelschlager

Albany, NY: Guha and Karthik Bala

Amherst, MA: Michael Kittredge

Anchorage, AK: Robert Gillam

Anderson, CA: Archie "Red" Emmerson

Atlanta, GA: Bernard Marcus

Austin, TX: Michael Dell

Baltimore, MD: Stephen Bisciotti

Bangor, ME: Stephen King

Belspring, VA: Randal J. "RJ" Kirk

Birmingham, AL: Miller Gorrie

Boston, MA: Peter M. Nicholas

Boulder, CO: Judi Paul

Buffalo, NY: Robert Wilmers

Burlington, VT: Robert Stiller

Carrollton, GA: Robert J. Stone

Charlotte, NC: O. Bruton Smith

Chicago, IL: Sam Zell

Cleveland, OH: A. Malachi Mixon

Cleveland, TN: W. Allan Jones

Colorado Springs, CO: Leroy Landhuis

Columbia, SC: Joe E. Taylor

Columbus, OH: Leslie H. Wexner

Dallas, TX: Harold C. Simmons

Danbury, CT: Fred DeLuca

Dayton, OH: Clayton H. Mathile

Daytona Beach, FL: Ron Rice

Denver, CO: Charles W. Ergen

Des Moines, IA (Ankeny): Dennis Albaugh

Detroit, MI: William Davidson

El Paso, TX: William D. Sanders

Fargo, ND: Gary Tharaldson

Fisher Island, FL: Bharat Desai

Fort Lauderdale, FL: Wayne Huizenga

Fort Worth, TX: David Bonderman

Fresno, CA: David McDonald

Grand Rapids, MI: Richard DeVos

Greenville, SC: Leighton Cubbage

Greenwich, CT: Thomas Peterffy

Harrisburg, PA: Alex Hartzler

Hartford, CT: Ronald Williams

Hollis, NH: Patrick McGovern

Honolulu, HI: Jay H. Shidler

Houston, TX: Dan Duncan

Indianapolis, IN: Christel DeHaan

Kansas City, KS: Min Kao

Kansas City, MO: James E. Stowers

Knoxville, TN: James A. Haslam II

Lake Charles, LA: William J. Doré

Las Vegas, NV: Sheldon Adelson

Little Rock, AR: Frank Hickingbotham

Livonia, MI: Danny Gilbert

Los Angeles, CA: Kirk Kerkorian

Louisville, KY: David A. Jones Sr.

Madison, WI: Pleasant Rowland

Memphis, TN: Frederick W. Smith

Meridian, MS: Hartley Peavey

Miami, FL: Jorge Pérez

Milwaukee, WI: William Kellogg

Minneapolis, MN: Richard Schulze

Missoula, MT: Dennis Washington

Morgantown, WV: Milan "Mike" Puskar

Nashville, TN: Thomas F. Frist Jr.

Newport Beach, CA: Donald Bren

New York, NY: Carl Icahn

Oklahoma City, OK: David Green

Omaha, NE: J. Joseph Ricketts

Orlando, FL: Harris Rosen

Palo Alto, CA: Sergey Brin

Pensacola, FL: Fredric Levin

Philadelphia, PA: Josh Kopelman

Portland, ME: Roxanne Quimby

Portland, OR: Phillip Knight

Providence, RI: Jonathan Nelson

Raleigh, NC: O. Temple Sloan Jr.

Rochester, NY: Thomas Golisano

Rodeo, NM: John McAfee

Sacramento, CA: Marvin "Buzz" Oates

Salt Lake City, UT: Jon Meade Huntsman Sr.

San Antonio, TX: Billy Joe "Red" McCombs

San Diego, CA: Charles Brandes

Sandpoint, ID: Dennis Pence

San Francisco, CA: Larry Page

Savannah, GA: Robert Jepson Jr.

Scottsdale, AZ: Bruce Halle

Seattle, WA: William Gates III

Sioux City, SD: Denny Sanford

Spartanburg, SC: George Johnson

Spokane, WA: Harlan D. Douglass

St. Louis, MO: Jack Taylor

Syracuse, NY: Robert J. Congel

Toledo, OH: Paul Ormond

Trenton, NJ: Jon Corzine

Tucson, AZ: Jim Click

Tuscaloosa, AL: James I. Harrison Jr.

Washington, DC: David Rubenstein

Wichita, KS: Phillip Ruffin

Wilmington, DE: Charles Cawley

Woodside, CA: Larry Ellison

PART II

HOW THEY DID IT:
THE TWELVE COMMANDMENTS
OF WEALTH

RMIT Commandment #1

SEEK MONEY FOR MONEY'S SAKE AND YE SHALL NOT FIND

Money will only come when you are doing the right thing in the right way.

—Randal J. Kirk

In virtually every discussion I had with America's RMITs, each would say, in one form or another, "It's not about the money." But this, I found, was one of the great lies that rich people tell themselves and anyone willing to listen. This belief—that it's not about the money—somehow makes ultra-affluent folks feel better about themselves. Maybe it helps assuage some misplaced guilt. At least it makes them appear humble. After two years of similar discussions with these extraordinary individuals, I can tell you unequivocally it's very much about the money. But it's about the money only as the barometer of their success.

New York City's activist investor Carl Icahn, who has a net worth of $16 billion, says, "All humans collect something, I collect money. Money is the scorecard in business success." But he rightly points out that "to a world-class cellist, success is making it to Carnegie Hall." While Icahn is correct that there are many definitions of success, the one I will focus on is the success of wealth creation. Many RMITs were candid and admitted that growing up, they wanted to be rich, and often thought about having more abundance in their lives. Quite simply, they wanted to have a better life than they enjoyed during their youth.

Here's the startling and seemingly counterintuitive revelation that the majority of RMITs have experienced or observed along their unique journeys, however. If you seek money strictly for the sake of becoming rich, most likely you will never achieve true financial freedom. Ironically, great wealth most often comes to those who seek it least. If you seek wealth for wealth's sake, you're doomed to failure and destined for a life of little real worth or value. This is a philosophy that America's great successes embrace fervently. RMITs are staunch in their belief that you must first create substantial value—products or services that enhance people's lives—before the money will flow from any commercial enterprise. Only by creating value will you ever attract significant wealth. This is the first commandment of creating great wealth. Seek money for the sake of money alone and ye shall not find.

This common sentiment was summed up best by Randal J. "RJ" Kirk, the biotech billionaire from Belspring, Virginia. He said, "It's a Zen thing. If you seek money alone as your ultimate goal, you are almost assured of not receiving any." Kirk believes that money is a valuable tool and a very useful by-product of some highly valuable contribution you make to the universe. He counsels, "Never ever do anything only for money, period. If you find something you really love and that society finds valuable, then the money comes rather easily." Carl Icahn shares the most common philosophy I heard from RMITs: "Find something you love to do, that you are absolutely passionate about, and the money will come."

My initial reaction to the countless statements like Icahn's and RJ Kirk's was, *Well, yeah, that's easy for you to say as you sit comfortably upon your billion-dollar wallets*. My RMIT research reveals, however, that Kirk and Icahn are correct—it is the value you bring to a company, an organization, indeed, the universe, that ultimately determines your level of wealth. Kirk is right on the money when he says, "Money will come only when you are doing the right thing in the right way." He believes, like most RMITs, that accumulating wealth for the sake of wealth alone is self-defeating. In other words, it is the voyage that counts; it is the journey that produces the real pot of gold at the end of the rainbow.

Indianapolis's RWIT, Christel DeHaan, has learned that the critical lesson of wealth creation is to generate value first; money is the very pleasant by-product. She has experienced the ultimate American Dream, even though it all began in her native Germany. To develop her English-language skills, she left home at sixteen to be a nanny in England. She later returned to Germany and worked for the American armed forces as a translator. There she met and married an American soldier, who brought her to Indianapolis. With two young children and in need of extra income, she ran a typing service from her home. She says, "For me, I never thought about the desire for money or great wealth, I never thought about coming to America to seek fame and fortune, I simply thought about the needs of my family and I did what I needed to do to help provide for them."

From this modest beginning, DeHaan, only a decade later, was running a multinational company, Resort Condominiums International, with offices around the world. She received her just remuneration when she sold the company for $825 million to Henry Silverman's Cendant Corporation. She never sought the money for money's sake, but she agrees that the well-earned wealth is a powerful side effect of her toil and her ambition. She says, "I never wanted to sit still, I never wanted to accept the status quo. I had the ambition to finish what I had started. The reward simply came as a result of those efforts."

The Existential Question: Does Money Buy Happiness?

Don't get me wrong: RMITs very much enjoy the fruits of their labor. Ron Rice of Daytona Beach, Florida, who created his fortune by starting Hawaiian Tropic, candidly admits, "I love money, I love the freedom it affords, I love the reward that it demonstrates, and I love what I can do with it to enjoy my life more abundantly." Bill Doré of Lake Charles, Louisiana, who built Global Industries from the deep sea up, says, "I'm proud of my scorecard." A $700 million score is indeed something to be proud of, but he emphasizes that the passion for his business, the thrill of the hunt, and his incremental approach to building his businesses and his wealth encouraged him to enjoy the money, too. He recalls, "I woke up one day when I was thirty-two years old and my accountant said, 'Bill, you're worth a million dollars.'" He said to his accountant, "Well, I've got to go out and celebrate!" And celebrate he did.

That evening he took his wife, Kay, his parents, and his in-laws out for a big I'm-a-millionaire-now dinner. "It was a profound moment for me, and yet I never set out to reach that milestone. When I started out, all I wanted was to be incrementally better off than I was the year before. I never said to myself, *I want to be a multimillionaire*," he says. "I just wanted to earn another 10 cents an hour. I just wanted constant incremental progress." *The Richest Man in Town* proves that money does indeed translate to happiness. *But only when it is self-earned, when it is a direct result of effort by you—not money simply bestowed upon you.* It brings happiness when the wealth is the result of real value that you have added to the world in some important way. Happiness is a uniquely subjective experience. Still, I asked each RMIT: "After all that you have achieved, experienced, and mastered, are you truly happy?" And to a person, they offered a resounding yes. RMITs love the lives they have created for themselves.

One of the most memorably happy responses was from Jim

Harrison, the titan of Tuscaloosa, Alabama. Harrison took one drugstore in a small Alabama town and turned it into one of the largest pharmacy chains in America before selling to Rite Aid in 1997, yielding a multimillion-dollar wealth benefit. He says, "I'm the happiest guy on earth. I have a great family, I have had three great companies, and with my foundation work today, I'm doing something I love more than anything I have ever done in my life." The Harrisons of Tuscaloosa are referred to as the First Family of Pharmacy in Alabama. Commenting on the windfall he received after nearly a lifetime of building these companies, Harrison says, "The money is great because it buys you freedom, but what really makes me happy is making a difference." He's making himself happy because he's affecting the lives of so many others through his family foundation, but I sense that Harrison, like most RMITs, is the kind of guy who'd be happy even if he weren't so successful.

Jim Oelschlager is the richest man in Akron, Ohio, in the most holistic sense of the word *rich*. He is also, perhaps, the happiest man I met during this journey. "I wake up each day happy to be alive and proud to be an American," he says, "because in America, each of us has the right to pursue happiness. It is, of course, up to you to make your own success and happiness. Happiness is not guaranteed, but the right to pursue it sure is." Thomas Jefferson was right when he wrote the Declaration of Independence guaranteeing this inalienable right. Happiness, not money, should be the greatest reward of success—and for these extraordinary folks, it is. Oelschlager plays without complaint the cards he was dealt, which include being wheelchair-bound by multiple sclerosis. "I have been dealt a good hand," he says, "and my advice has always been to play your good cards." Despite his physical limitations, he has built a hugely successful investment company, Oak Associates, with $30 billion of assets under management. He has also built a fortune of several hundred million dollars—and a life that is truly admirable.

For Omaha, Nebraska's Joe Ricketts, every statement exudes happiness. "I'm happier today than anytime in my life, but I credit my mom with always holding out as positive examples those people who achieved a lot in life, whether in business, music, sports, or virtually any endeavor." His online trading company, TD Ameritrade, might have put a billion bucks in his pocket, but it was he who put the happiness in his life.

While we know that money cannot literally purchase happiness, the hard cold fact is that people with significant wealth are almost always happier than those with less in the bank—and especially when the fortune is of their own making. There are people who have loads of money—and there are people who are rich—and there is a decided difference between them. RMITs, it seems, are rich in the healthiest sense of the term. Robert Gillam, the richest man in Anchorage, Alaska—indeed, the richest man in the entire state—says, "I love my life. I can't wait to get up every morning and fire up my computer and think about where the opportunities are today. I love the adventure of life."

So why, then, are these people so happy? My conclusion is that they take personal responsibility for their happiness, just as they take personal responsibility for their businesses, their failures, and their lives. There are no excuses for RMITs. They seek to make a difference in the world, and the money is both the reward for their worthy contributions and the means to carry their dreams and their enterprises farther.

Roxanne Quimby of Portland, Maine, is the genius who colonized Burt's Bees, the enormously successful environmentally conscious consumer products company that she co-founded and then sold to Clorox, reaping a honey pot in excess of $300 million. "Abraham Lincoln was right when he said, 'Most people are about as happy as they make up their minds to be,'" she declares. "I would add that most people are as happy as they are happy with their work."

Wayne Huizenga, the richest man in Fort Lauderdale, Florida, is one of the greatest value builders of the twentieth and twenty-first centuries. He also sees hard work as the key to fulfillment. When he was selling the video rental company Blockbuster to Viacom, he said, "We had an atmosphere where everybody was happy. We were building a great enterprise, something of real value, and that makes people happy. And the money certainly didn't make them unhappy."

Most modern economists who have studied the subject of money and happiness agree. Most recently, economists Betsey Stevenson and Justin Wolfers of the University of Pennsylvania presented a study at the Brookings Institution in Washington, DC, that corroborates what all these richest men and women in town have been saying. According to Stevenson and Wolfers, as cited by the *New York Times*, 90 percent of the households in America that have incomes of $250,000 or more call themselves "very happy." The key to achieving both money *and* happiness is to remember which is the cause and which is the effect. That is precisely what all these RMITs did—they made it themselves.

When Christel DeHaan gave the 2008 commencement address at the University of Indianapolis—where she chairs the board of trustees—she cited a study done of lottery winners conducted by Northwestern University. The study found that the winners of those big lottery windfalls were no happier than nonwinners. But in truth, this isn't surprising at all, given that lottery winners are just like inheritors of great wealth—they didn't earn the money, they simply lucked into it. Indeed, the common theme of these RMITs—that part of the great satisfaction of being successful was how hard they worked along the way—plays a significant role in their happiness in life.

John McAfee, the anti-computer-virus king of Rodeo, New Mexico, probably has a half-billion-dollar fortune, and he sees the world through his own unique lens. "People think that if you have lots of money, then your life is set," he says, "and for me, that is definitely not true." One of the absurdities of

McAfee's life with wealth was the acquisition of what he simply calls "stuff." "Financial success brings many things to our lives," he says, "it brings freedom, attention—sometimes unwanted attention—and, yes, it inevitably brings stuff. Stuff that we don't need, stuff simply to fill some gaping hole within ourselves that can't be filled with, well, stuff." McAfee is not suggesting that money is evil, that it is something to be avoided. All RMITs agree that money is a good thing, but it must be earned and used well in order to bring any degree of real happiness into your life. McAfee agrees with the late comedian George Carlin, who famously said a house is just "a place to keep your stuff while you go out and get more stuff." McAfee offers, "If I had my life to do all over again, I would have done it with less stuff and more grace, meaning being less driven by the urge to meet society's measure of success and more driven by the urge to integrate the world around me through my company in a harmonious way."

His New Age sensibility is really not that different from what *Great Gatsby* author F. Scott Fitzgerald expressed when he wrote, "Once one is caught up into the material world, not one person in ten thousand finds the time to form literary taste, to examine the validity of philosophic concepts for himself, or to form what, for lack of a better phrase, I might call the wise and tragic sense of life." In his early sixties now, McAfee sold his company—whose products are most likely protecting your computer from nasty viruses—and he has time for some serious introspection as he builds a new town and a new life in the desert of New Mexico.

This RMIT happiness, then, seems to stem not just from having a copious amount of money, certainly not from seeking money for money's sake, but rather from creating real value in the world and from the joys of the journey to such stealth-like success. Granted, the rich and successful may have deeper worries and greater responsibilities that are part and parcel of significant wealth, but there is also security, belonging, self-esteem, and an opportunity for self-actualization—a virtual perfect pyramid of Abraham Maslow's hierarchy of needs. If our needs, wants, and desires are met, usually the result is that we find ourselves healthier (mentally and physically) and much happier. Success and the resultant wealth, then, buy the freedom to pursue true self-actualization. McAfee concedes that it is hard to eschew society's measures of success, but without a doubt he has figured out what is important to him, what brings him joy and happiness. Is he happy? He says, "Hell yes!" McAfee has found self-actualization in his new life, in his new town.

McAfee sold his interest in his namesake company for an estimated $150 million in 1999. Like many recipients of financial windfalls, he moved on to new opportunities. Those opportunities were far from Silicon Valley. He taught yoga; he launched a company called Tribal (which he later sold for $17 million, according to the *Wall Street Journal*); he built a state-of-the-art, ten-thousand-square-foot home overlooking Pikes Peak in Woodland Park, Colorado. Ever the seeker, once he had his epiphany that there was more to life than big homes and the stuff to fill them, he picked up and moved to Rodeo, New Mexico. He held a free yard sale and says, "I probably gave away a million dollars' worth of stuff." Reportedly very nice stuff. In his new town, he co-founded Sky Gypsies, a company (*club* would be more like it) of open-cockpit kite-wing plane lovers. These big-boy toy planes allow you to soar above the bucolic terrain and painted canyons of New Mexico and Arizona. You aerotrek just feet above the ground, where McAfee claims you can smell the grass or the scent of roaming cattle just as the birds can. He has spent millions to build airstrips in several locations across New Mexico and Arizona to allow his passion to take flight. He has not only conceived a new sport and a new business, but also built a new town—a desert town with a movie theater and a coffee shop serving the latest in lattes. This new passion, avocation, and now vocation brings new meaning to the word *freedom*. He is living the life that American poet Robert Frost advocated when he wrote in "Two Tramps in Mud Time,"

> *My object in living is to unite.*
> *My avocation and my vocation*
> *As my two eyes make one in sight.*

RMITs find a way to unite their avocation with their vocation—a sure-fire recipe for both happiness and wealth creation.

Can RMITs Ever Be Satisfied?

RMITs are clearly happy. They are enjoying the journey; they have reveled in their contributions. But are they ever truly content? The short answer is no. Just because RMITs are happy does not mean they are satisfied. McAfee is just one such story of an RMIT who continues to seek. RMITs are insatiable questers, always searching for that next mountain to climb or canyon to soar above. This makes sense; as Dr. Rob Reiner, a psychologist from New York University Medical Center, is fond of saying: "We're neurologically wired to never be content." If we were, we wouldn't have anything to strive for, and RMITs are nothing if not strivers. Private equity powerhouse David Rubenstein of the Carlyle Group in Washington, DC, would no doubt agree. Despite a net worth of billions, he jokes, "I'm Jewish and I'm not supposed to be happy. It would make me unhappy to be happy, because I would realize that I'm not trying hard enough." Like Rubenstein, RMITs simply can never be totally satisfied because feeling satisfied, in their minds, would signal that the game is over. They never want the game to end. But how much money does it take for RMITs to feel at least a semblance of contentment? Rubenstein cites Felix Rohatyn's famous answer when the former ambassador to France and managing director of Lazard Frères was asked, "How much money does it take to feel truly secure?" The man who is widely credited with averting New

York City's plunge into bankruptcy in the 1970s replied, "Twice as much as you currently have." The not-so-subtle implication being that most RMITs need twice as much as they have, because they believe they still have so much to accomplish. The journey doesn't end until, well, life ends.

The RMIT of Hollis, New Hampshire, IDG founder Pat McGovern, says, "I believe in the Buddhist philosophy that the journey is the reward." McGovern's journey has been mighty rewarding, and it is an expedition that he does not want to end. He founded IDG, the world's leading technology publishing, research, and event management company, in 1964. Today McGovern's privately held company has revenues in excess of $3 billion, and he has no desire to sell it. He says, "Why would I want something to end that is so much fun and continues to bring me such pleasure and such rewards?" Hartley Peavey, the music maestro of Meridian, Mississippi, who has created one of the most recognizable names in electronic amplification technology, couldn't agree more. "When we had Peavey's fortieth anniversary," he says, "a friend and colleague wanted to write a book about the success of the company, and I said, 'You can't do that because the story is far from over, the fat lady certainly hasn't sung.'" The fat lady never sings for RMITs. They never stop to rest on their laurels, not even on major anniversaries. That seemingly never-ending quest *is* what makes them happy.

So How Much Is Enough?

When interviewed, America's RMITs all, in some way, stated that great wealth was never their primary motivation. Money, however, is still the scoreboard for most truly successful people. An occasional glance at that scoreboard of success brings RMITs a serious degree of delight, if not total contentment, as they see their tally rise. But even if RMITs don't want the game to end, how do they know when they've won?

It's the age-old question, "How much money is enough?" A

few years ago, I wrote a column in *Worth* magazine by this title. It was a question that I was asking myself personally, and many of my friends were thinking about it as well. No doubt the answer is deceptively simple, but also deeply personal—one that can only come from within. To find my personal answer, I began to read a lot on the topic. I also began to ask my friends that question, and to listen more intently to the experience of others far wiser than I am.

On Christmas Eve a few years ago, my wife and I were at a party that the noted author Gay Talese and his editor wife, Nan, give annually. The Talese party always brings out the most glittering of the literati. At one point, Connie and I found ourselves chatting with novelist Kurt Vonnegut, and I casually asked Kurt what he was currently working on. He proceeded to tell us that he had just finished a poem that was soon to appear in *The New Yorker* about a great insight he had gained from his old friend, *Catch-22* author Joseph Heller. Vonnegut told the story of being at the home of an unnamed billionaire with Heller one evening when Joe said, "Kurt, I have something that our host can never have." Vonnegut, basking in all the grandeur of the surroundings, said, "And what is that, Joe?" Heller replied, "The knowledge that I have enough." With that insight, Heller had perfectly defined *rich*.

Write Your Own Obituary

What amount makes you rich enough, then, is a very personal decision, not a townwide competition. In that *Worth* column, I suggested that the best way to make this personal assessment is to write your own obituary. As morbid as that may sound, it's one of the most enlightening exercises I have ever experienced. To be sure, none of us really wants to think about the end of our lives. It's daunting to imagine what will be said when the curtain comes down on our last act. But that being said, it's a darn good way to plan the rest of your life. It's a magnificent and exacting lens through which to make the big decisions. It's also the perfect way to determine the answer to that critical question, "How much is enough?"

When I tried this exercise, I stared at a blank sheet of paper for what seemed like hours, and then it suddenly began to flow. I started with the accomplishments I am most proud of in my life. Then I considered the things for which I'm most grateful. This prepared me to give serious thought to what I still wanted to accomplish. I thought about the friendships I want to nurture, the hopes and dreams I have for my family, the places in the world I still want to experience. Immediately, I began to see patterns. I began to see how much work I still have to do. I realized that my life is so much more than my résumé and considerably more than my bank account. And I began to formulate an idea of how much wealth it would take for me to have the rich and full life that I envisioned. Try it. Write your own obituary. As odd as it sounds, I predict it will actually make you feel better. It will focus your efforts, force you to take the long view, and most likely cause you to change some things in your life. Here's how.

How to Write Your Own Obituary

Begin at the beginning—when and where you were born. Think about your most meaningful childhood memories and the greatest lessons of your formative years. Think about your high school and college accomplishments. A healthy dose of self-deprecating humor can make this exercise quite fun. Write about your first job. Reflect on the relationships that have helped to define your life. Another way of looking at this exercise is to think of it as a condensed autobiography. Write about your greatest triumphs. Think through the most difficult periods of your life and the lessons learned. None of us lives a life free of pain. (See RMIT Commandment #7, Fail to Succeed.) Face your failures head-on, and think through the gifts that eventually came into your life because of those tough trials. Weave them into your life story.

Now think through your hopes and dreams for the future—what you still want to accomplish in your life, places you still dream of visiting, experiences that capture your interest and imagination, books you still want to read, and people you want to get to know. And last, think how you wish to be remembered. What would you like engraved on your tombstone? My favorite epitaph is the one Malcolm Forbes wrote for himself: "While Alive, He Lived." My personal choice is, "He Made a Difference." I decided on this many years ago when toiling at *Esquire* magazine as we were producing a special fiftieth-anniversary issue called 50 Who Made a Difference. It was a celebration and acknowledgment of fifty people who over the fifty years of the magazine's existence had profoundly changed the way we as a society view the world. It was a tip of the *Esquire* hat to the belief that, as Phillip Moffitt said then, "All that comprises any society is a network of individual action." The fifty individuals chosen—ranging from Jonas Salk to Jackie Robinson, from Neil Armstrong to Thomas Watson—made an indelible mark on the American landscape. I was not grandiose enough in my thought process then, or now, to think I could or would do something that would have the impact of these great individuals, but I did know one thing—somehow I wanted to make a difference.

That epitaph has been my constant guide and inspiration. It has shepherded me through many difficult decisions and more than a few hard times. Your epitaph decision should help you make a lot of the hard decisions in life. Thankfully, I've still got time to work on living up to mine. To see how I completed the obituary exercise—or simply for a bit of inspiration, or a potential personal obituary template—visit www.richestmanintown.com and click on RANDY'S FUTURE OBITUARY.

The Journey or the Pot of Gold

Near the end of my interview with Miami's main man, Jorge Pérez, the real estate developer and owner of The Related Group, I asked what he would call his proudest business accomplishment—his greatest success. After reflecting for a moment, he said, "The next one, because the joy is in the creation, the joy is in the journey."

Indeed, one question that arose again and again in the course of my interviews with the richest persons in a hundred American towns was that very one: "Which brought you greater happiness—the journey or the actual arrival at destination success?" Without fail, the richest men and women in town responded that they most valued and most enjoyed the journey. Like most RMITs, Pérez says, "I'm the sort of guy who is never satisfied, but that doesn't mean that I'm not happy. I have a great wife, four incredible kids, a partner with great integrity, beautiful homes, but I know there is so much more I can and must do. I am always being challenged by myself." He never sought the wealth simply to be rich. Pérez sought to build a luxury real estate business that would benefit from his perfectionist personality. The money simply followed. RMITs encourage us to seek the journey, not the cash. They encourage us to make a valuable contribution to the world. The money is the reward for having made a real difference.

- Seek money for money's sake—and it will elude you.
- Wealth comes as the result of contributing real value.
- Money does buy happiness, but only if it's self-made.
- Write your own obituary.
- Remember, the joy is in the journey.

RMIT Commandment #2

FIND YOUR PERFECT PITCH

Knowing others is intelligence; knowing yourself is true wisdom. Mastering others is strength; mastering yourself is true power.

—Tao Te Ching

One thing all RMITs have in common is that they know who they are—they have a keen sense of what makes them tick, they understand their own motivations, and most have mastered the difficult task of deciphering their greatest talents and abilities. In short, they have developed self-knowledge. Neuroscientists tell us that we are all hardwired with certain aptitudes, talents, interests, and inclinations. RMITs seem to know this instinctively. They know that personal assessment is the first step to wealth amassment.

Did your parents or loved ones ever say to you, "You can do anything you put your mind to"? "You can be anything you dream of being"? Brace yourself—they lied to you. These were not deliberate lies, of course. They simply meant to encourage you. The truth is, RMITs do not believe that you can be anything that you put your mind to. You cannot do anything and everything that your mind can imagine. But this is good news. This revelation is liberating because it frees you to be so much more of what you innately, intrinsically, instinctively are. No matter what your level of ability, no matter what talents you innately possess, you have within you more potential to develop those talents than you can possibly explore in a lifetime. Although your talents, abilities, and proclivities are as unique to you as your DNA—and therefore finite—the possibilities for exploiting, developing, and commercializing those unique talents are limitless.

Finding your own unique gifts is the second step to becoming the richest man in town. You must determine what Jim Haslam of Knoxville, Tennessee, the chairman of Pilot Oil, refers to as "what is right about you." He says, "I don't care what anybody says. Anybody who has been successful has gotten into a business that suits their personality and their skill sets. If you think you *have* to go to work each day—you've got the wrong job." Haslam is right. You have to find what is right about yourself, and then work isn't work, it's pleasure. It's all too easy for us to discern what is wrong with ourselves at times, and even easier to see what is wrong with others, but America's RMITs prove that you must not let what you cannot do interfere with what you *can* do—*what you are uniquely gifted to do*. Focusing on your limitations will not make you the richest man in town—but accentuating your own innate abilities will. Warren Buffett once told *Fortune* magazine, "When we got married in 1952, I told Susie [Buffett's first wife] I was going to be rich. That wasn't going to be because of any special virtues of mine or even because of hard work, but simply because I was born with the right skills, in the right place at the right time. I was wired at birth to allocate capital." Like Warren Buffett, we are all hardwired to do something. Figuring out what that is, is the key to knowing yourself and unlocking your full potential.

W. Clement Stone, who in his day was the richest man in

Chicago, a famous insurance executive, and author of numerous books on success, once observed, "Whatever the mind of man can conceive, it can achieve." This ditty sounds good on the surface, but—with all due respect to Stone, who was highly successful—today's RMITs prove this long-held theory woefully wrong. RMITs believe that you cannot be anything you conceive or believe. You cannot be anything your loved ones believe you can be. However, RMITs attest that you can be so much more of who you instinctively, intrinsically, rightfully, and genetically are. Warren Buffett knew he was wired to be an investor, an allocator of capital. He recognized his unique gifts, his innate talents—he knew himself. Sixty-two billion dollars later, I think he has proved the precept.

Jonathan Nelson, the CEO of Providence Equity Partners and the richest man in Providence, Rhode Island, learned the critical know-thyself lesson while taking a course on Beethoven at Brown University. "I knew very little about classical music when I signed up for the class, and it is safe to say I still know little about classical music. I thought it might be fun and easy. There was nothing more to it than that. On the first day of class, our instructor played a few notes and asked the class who could identify the notes. It was a small class and it seemed to me about 25 percent of the class had their hand up. I was not among them. The professor called on someone: 'C-sharp,' the student responded. How, the professor asked, did he know that? 'I have perfect pitch,' said the student. It turns out that was the only way to know the key. Those students with their hands up all had perfect pitch.

"Well . . . . I knew two things at that moment. First, 25 percent of the class had a significant advantage over me. They had a talent I could not acquire and it made them better equipped than I to do well in the class. Second, I realized that this class would not be easy for me to ace—now I was worried about passing. But I stayed with it. I barely passed. I learned about Beethoven and an unfamiliar musical genre, and I developed an appreciation for the power of relative skill differences. Or maybe it was just fun to learn and spend time with people who were much better at something than me. Even if I knew then where I wanted to be in ten years, this class would not have directly helped me get there. But I did learn the lifelong lesson that while perfect pitch is a real talent, so, too, is recognizing one's relative skills and abilities."

Nelson practices what he learned in that fateful class at Brown, and it has served him well. Worth at least $2 billion, he is not only the richest man in Providence; he is the wealthiest man in the entire state. To illustrate this idea of perfect pitch, he tells the story of the revitalization of James Bond: "When we acquired the movie studio MGM two years ago, the big question was, What would we do with James Bond—who will be the next Bond? This is one case where the human interest lined up with the financial significance. MGM actually owns the Bond franchise with a brother-and-sister team who are the offspring of Cubby Broccoli, the creator of the James Bond franchise. Barbara Broccoli and her late father had already endured many studio chiefs along the way to successfully producing twenty-one Bond flicks. Before we closed the MGM deal, we insisted on meeting with Barbara, who was to be our new partner in the company's—if not the industry's—most important movie franchise. We had key decisions to make and we needed to come to an agreement quickly.

"Barbara was like one of the kids in class with perfect pitch. I said we were not here to approve scripts or select the next Bond. She could do that unencumbered by our ownership. We took a big risk. The movie took the franchise in a new direction. And the much-maligned Bond choice, Daniel Craig, became an overnight sensation and was met with universal support from the critics. I am here to say that we deserve none of the credit. Barbara had the 'perfect pitch' for Bond. Recognizing and respecting those skills was a lesson learned in that first day of the Beethoven course."

Nelson's point is clear: No amount of positive thinking or wishful willing can make you something you are not. Lose the misconception that you can be anything you set your mind to. Instead, work to your strengths: Decide what is right with you. Stephen King, the richest man in Bangor, Maine, and perhaps the most commercially successful writer in America, knew early in life what was right about himself. He has said, "There was nothing else I was made to do. I was made to write stories and I love to write stories. That's why I do it. I really can't imagine doing anything else and I can't imagine not doing what I do."

What Is Right with You?

Even Andrew Carnegie, best known as the second richest man in history, had it partially wrong, too. The steel magnate, who wrote "The Gospel of Wealth" in 1889, was famous for saying, "There is a power under your control that is greater than poverty, greater than the lack of education, greater than all your fears and superstitions combined. It is the power to take possession of your own mind and direct it to whatever ends you may desire." Each of us possesses incredible personal powers, and while there is no doubt that an optimistic, can-do spirit is important and belief in yourself is critical to success and wealth creation, your potential is limitless only when you find and use those powers that form your own perfect pitch. Finding it is essential, and that requires some serious introspection and a truly honest assessment of your talents and abilities. You must focus intently on your individual strengths and talents—what is right about you.

Birmingham, Alabama's construction czar Miller Gorrie knew what was right about him from an early age. "I always knew that I wanted to be in the construction business," he says. "I couldn't imagine anything else." The son of an IBM salesperson, he remembers his father telling him the story of when Tom Watson, the founder of IBM, came to their home for dinner one evening when Gorrie was only eight years old. To show his appreciation for the nice home-cooked meal, Watson reached into his pocket to give some money to young Gorrie and his brother. He says, "My father says that my brother went for the change. But I grabbed the bills." Gorrie spent three years in the navy's Civil Engineering Corps after graduating from Auburn University in 1957. When he started out, he was frustrated: "No one else was willing to pay me what I deserved, so I bought my own company." Gorrie found his perfect pitch early in life—and what's more, he knew just how much that was worth.

Dayton, Ohio, farm boy billionaire Clay Mathile took longer to find his calling. He recalls how lucky he was to be awarded a full scholarship by the basketball coach at Ohio Northern University since he could not afford the tuition. He played well during his freshman year, and was praised highly by his coach. In fact, at the spring athletic banquet the coach said that Mathile had the potential to be one of the best guards the school had ever seen. But then, unexpectedly, the coach reneged on his promise and gave Mathile's scholarship to an incoming freshman that summer. The betrayal hurt at the time, but in retrospect Mathile says, "The coach did me a major favor because I was never going to make my living playing basketball."

Basketball was not his perfect pitch; running businesses, however, was. Mathile walked away from his first post-college job at Campbell Soup and took a chance on a small pet foods company started by pet lover Paul Iams. Mathile took sole ownership of the Iams company in 1982 and built it into a billion-dollar organization, which he sold to Procter and Gamble in 1999 for $2.3 billion. He even earmarked $100 million of the sale proceeds to go to his loyal employees.

Hartley Peavey, the music man of Meridian, Mississippi, always had a passion for playing guitar. "I saw Bo Diddley in 1957," he says, "and I went wild. I wanted more than anything to be a great guitar star, and I tried for the next eight years to be just that, but the sad fact was that I was probably one of the world's worst guitar players. I had to face myself in the mirror and say that I was not going to be a rock star." That realization prompted some serious thought. "A funny thing happened along the way. I learned that I was pretty damn good at building things. So I started thinking about what I loved and what I was good at." In his junior year of college, he says, "I had an intervention with myself and said if I can't be the world's greatest guitar player, maybe I can build the amplifiers that make the best musicians sound even better." Peavey discovered what is undeniably one of the top tenets of RMIT success: Know thyself. *You must have the courage to make a truly honest assessment of your unique talents and abilities, then match those with your personal passions and interests.* The exercise is not as simple as it sounds. Recognizing our true strengths means recognizing what we lack—letting go perhaps of some unattainable, unfortunate dreams.

Personal Lies

According to Hartley Peavey, "We are so good at lying to ourselves about our talents and innate strengths that there is a word for it—and it's called rationalization." He remembers his personal lie well. "I was saying to myself, 'If only I had a seventy-watt amp rather than a thirty-five-watt amp, then maybe I would sound better.' But the reality was that I was just a louder awful guitar player." By being honest with himself, by refusing to rationalize any longer, he led himself to his true calling: to build one of the largest music electronics firms in the world. Peavey's company pioneered computer-controlled machining in the making of high-quality, affordable guitars. It also manufactures amplifiers, speakers, and music software so that hundreds of thousands of bands can pursue their musical passions. Peavey found the perfect way to marry his passion with his unique talents and abilities; as a result, he holds more than 130 patents and has built a $500 million company, which he controls 100 percent. Now in his midsixties, he shows no signs of slowing down, because he is as passionate today about music, and building the equipment to produce and enjoy it, as he was when Bo Diddley first blew his mind.

Peavey has always marched to his own tune. "By definition, you cannot be the best and be just like everybody else," he says. "To dare to be different is easy to say, but damn difficult to do. Most people simply don't have the cojones to be different." Peavey is right: Following your unique talents sometimes means blazing a trail into the unknown. He continues, "People are always looking for the secret recipe to success and wealth creation and they are almost always looking for that recipe from without. The recipe is actually within—it's inside of all of us. You just have to know how to reach in there and grab it. The reality is that we all come into this world with our own unique bag of tricks. Some people call them talents, abilities, proclivities—it doesn't matter what the moniker is. The truth is, we are all different. We have to understand those unique differences and not only celebrate them, but employ them in our pursuit of happiness, success, and wealth."

Peavey thinks that most Americans—most people of the world, in fact—get caught up in the concept that we all are born equal. He proffers, "In the eyes of the law and in the eyes of God, I guess we are all born equal, but thank God we are not all born the same." Discovering and honing your unique talents is the most important step to becoming the richest man in town.

If It Feels Good, Do It

Many people have not mastered the art of finding their perfect pitch. You are a natural at something. Some things simply come easier for you than other things. What are those things? Think about what you do best. Ask yourself the question: *What would I do if I knew I couldn't fail?* Ponder what puts a smile on your face, what makes time fly because you're having so much fun. Stay away from those things that don't bring you joy and excitement, that aren't of interest to you, that don't make your heart race like your first crush. If you're not a numbers person, then obviously you shouldn't be pursuing accounting. If you have no sense of style, then you shouldn't be an interior decorator or fashion designer. If you aren't good at basketball, don't dream of your day in the NBA. RMITs systematically divest themselves of the things they don't naturally excel at, enjoy, or find emotionally or intellectually stimulating. They seek more pleasure, less pain.

Fred Levin, a flamboyant personal injury attorney and the richest man in Pensacola, Florida, says, "Taking the path of least resistance is the surest way to finding your pathway to success." That seems counterintuitive, almost anti-American, but RMITs prove it is true. Levin never doubted for a moment what his pathway to success and wealth was to be. He wanted to be a trial attorney. Now Florida's most successful trial attorney, having won hundreds of millions from the tobacco companies, Levin says, "While this may be counter to what most of us grow up hearing from family and friends, the old refrain *You can accomplish anything you set your mind to* . . . simply isn't true." It doesn't pay to become a Greek tragedy like Sisyphus, constantly pushing a boulder up the mountain only to see it cascade back down the hill. Levin, who loves a good fight (he has also served as the manager for boxing great Roy Jones Jr.), is right. Why struggle pushing a rock uphill when, instead, you can have the wind at your back? Levin knows what things make him tick, and getting attention is one of those things. His talent for self-promotion is very much a part of his perfect pitch. Despite his controversial reputation, his name sits atop his alma mater—and the state's most prestigious—law school, the University of Florida. This king of torts figured out his unique talents and abilities and followed them not to the orchestra hall or into a university classroom, but into the courtroom and before the camera.

Part of the Puritan work ethic instilled in most of us is the belief that we must work hard to overcome our weaknesses, that we must face our deficits head-on and attack them with near-fanatical fervor. That's not the runway to runaway success, however. RMITs have become the richest men and women in their towns because they have assessed their unique talents and nurtured their distinctive strengths. They accentuate their own positive traits, talents, and innate skills. Bill Gates once noted, "Early in the history of Microsoft, our view was, if you were very smart then you could learn how to manage people, how to do business, how to do marketing. It turns out that talent isn't that fungible. Somebody who is great at doing software in many ways is often not the right person to manage people."

Anti-virus virtuoso John McAfee said that it took him until his late forties to know himself fully. His best advice? "Find out who you are early; find out what you're best at and what you really want before you go out and try to achieve what the outside world has defined as success." You must make your own definition of success. McAfee says, "I simply bought lock, stock, and barrel what my parents told me was success—what the movies, TV, and all the books on success told me was success. I did that without regard to what success really meant to me."

In this post-software phase of his life, he has built his own town in the desert of New Mexico and a new business that combines his talent for building things and his passion for flying—in this case, flying kite-wing plane contraptions that look like motorcycles with wings. McAfee's Sky Gypsies is a band of brothers who share a love of navigating the canyons and crevices of New Mexico and Arizona in these one-person aerotrekking gliders. Soaring silently over the desert terrain allows for some serious and continuing soul searching—the kind of personal internal analysis that is a critical step to becoming the richest man in town.

None of this is to say that everyone is a hidden genius. You don't have to be a human calculator or a musical savant to have real, valuable, "monetizable" human capital. Billion-dollar Bob Gillam, the greatest success story in Anchorage, says, "It's not the Phi Beta Kappa who becomes the great change agent of the world. It's often the B student who has had to struggle—who knows what he is made of—who knows who he is." Gillam, a sixty-something Alaskan adventurer, exemplifies the Horatio Alger trajectory of so many RMITs. He began in modest circumstances, raised in the back room of his father's liquor store in Anchorage. He knew that he didn't want to run a liquor store, but he did love watching the way business works. He made his way from that storage room to one of the most prestigious business schools in America, the Wharton School of Business at the University of Pennsylvania. He struggled to get there, but he knew his calling was to be an investor and run his own company. He knew his perfect pitch. Like Nelson, Levin, Peavey, Mathile, and Gillam, you can only become an RMIT if you are performing from, and playing to, your personal strengths. Maya Angelou is right on the money: "You can only become truly accomplished at something you love. Don't make money your goal. Instead, pursue the things you love doing, and then do them so well that people can't take their eyes off you."

- You can't be something you're not . . . but you can be so much more of who you innately, intrinsically are. Everyone has his or her own unique perfect pitch.
- The path of least resistance is your surest road to success and sizable riches.
- How much you capitalize on your personal makeup ultimately determines how much capital you have in your personal wallet.
- What are you so good at that people can't take their eyes off you when you are doing it?

RMIT COMMANDMENT #3

BYOB: BE YOUR OWN BOSS

You don't get rich working for other people!

—Phil Ruffin

Find the founder in you: Build your own business, buy your own business, own your own business. If you hire yourself, you control your own life's direction. Like it or not, we live in a society in which there is no such thing as job security or a continual climb up the so-called corporate ladder. America's RMITs are prime examples. Ninety-four of the hundred RMITs have the title *founder* on their biographies—proof that it pays to hone the inner entrepreneur in you, even while you're working for someone else.

Richard DeVos Sr., who founded Amway along with high school best friend Jay Van Andel, said that his father encouraged him from his earliest youth to own his own business. Having lived through the Great Depression, DeVos's father knew that the only way to control your destiny is to own your own business and be your own boss. When asked if he ever considered taking the company public or selling, DeVos shot back, "No! For Jay and me, it was never about the money. It was about the thrill of owning our own business, controlling our own destinies." Even so, DeVos defines *success* as the "ability to improve the lives of others." He believes the best way to do that is by providing jobs and long-term security for a large group of employees—something he says a successful private company is best at doing.

Alex Hartzler of Harrisburg, Pennsylvania, was a corporate lawyer before becoming the man who helped build and ultimately sell the Internet marketing company Webclients to ValueClick for $141 million. Today Hartzler is a real estate developer and the most successful entrepreneur in Harrisburg. And he's still in his thirties. I asked him if he ever regretted leaving the stable legal profession for the turbulence of owning his own company. He said firmly, "Never! Law didn't afford me freedom, it didn't afford me ownership, and it didn't afford me the opportunity to enjoy the fruits of my labor." He has never looked back.

Dayton's Clayton Mathile had his I-must-own-my-own-business revelation while still in high school. A local farmer came to him and asked if he would be willing to tend his soybeans during the growing season. The farmer offered to pay him $10 a day; Mathile's good math skills told him that he could earn $800 by the end of the summer. "That was a lot of money in those days," he says. His father then made him a counterproposal, offering to give him eight acres of land to work, promising to provide him all the profits after the fall harvest. Mathile says, "I always thought, why work for the man when you can have the man work for you?" In late September, while young Mathile was at school, his father harvested the soybeans Clay had tended, combined them with his harvest, and promptly sold them at market. When Clay asked about his proceeds, his father sheepishly admitted that he had simply forgotten about their arrangement. Not surprisingly, he didn't have a particularly good relationship with his father after that breach of contract. He had long felt that his father's pessimism and conservatism kept him from achieving a richer, fuller, better life. And in the case of the forgotten soybean arrangement, his father had kept young Clay, too, from receiving the rewards of his efforts.

Mathile calls this deal his first real failure. He knew then that he couldn't work for his father, or anyone else for that matter, and vowed to own his own company one day. After the sale of Iams, Mathile wrote a book called *Dream No Little Dreams*, partially inspired by the sad fact that his father seemed to have had no dreams at all. Clay, however, sure did. He breathed life into his dream of a better existence, owning his own company and helping others in the process. Today, after his $2.3 billion sale of Iams, he spends most of his time at the Center for Entrepreneurial Education he started to help local entrepreneurs reach their own American Dream.

Less than 10 percent of America's RMITs have taken their companies public, and most cite the short-term thinking of Wall Street as a key reason. The more important reason, however, is that they lose control of their own destiny. RMITs trust themselves more than they trust anyone else to protect their companies, their wealth, and their futures. RMITs feel that when a company is forced to manage from quarter to quarter as opposed to taking a long-term view—employees often become viewed as commodities or overhead, not human beings and managers—then they spend too much of their time figuring out how to spin their stories to Wall Street as opposed to building their businesses. TD Ameritrade's Chairman Joe Ricketts needed new capital in 1997 to keep up with the explosive growth that the Internet was providing for his Omaha-based discount brokerage, so he took Ameritrade public on the NASDAQ exchange. He shares a common RMIT frustration, saying, "It's a distraction managing to the street's expectations and it's not fun for someone who is accustomed to running their own business. I didn't like it very much." Archie "Red" Emmerson, the largest landowner in California and the second largest in the United States (only an acre or two behind Ted Turner), took his company Sierra Pacific public in 1969, but he hated answering to Wall Street so much that he took the company private again five years later. He says simply, "I just like to work for myself."

One of the sometimes not-so-pretty truisms of capitalism is, "The new money calls the shots." It is not the creator of the innovative idea or the smart manager who builds an enterprise to outsize success who most often reaps the reward—it is the provider of the capital who gets massively rich if the enterprise is successful. That's why another maudlin maxim of capitalism is "Shoot the Founder." Often when a lone-ranger founder needs or—better put—is forced to raise capital to get his business off the ground or to scale up to the next level, he soon finds himself doing very little and having even less. When possible, RMITs believe that it is always better to self-finance your success, to remain your own boss, to control your own destiny.

I asked David Green, the humble owner of Hobby Lobby, if he would ever consider taking his family-owned multibillion-dollar company public. He said strongly, "I'm not interested. We don't need the cash. We are able to open twenty to thirty stores a year with our profits, and besides, I don't want to debate with stockholders about how we run our business or what we do with our profits." That wasn't always the case, however. Starting out making picture frames on their kitchen table, Green and his wife capitalized their business with a $600 loan. That loan, when it was paid off, allowed Green to stay firmly in control of his destiny. It allowed him to build a company with his values, not the values of Wall Street or outside investors. Green has been his own boss from the very beginning. Like all RMITs, he likes it that way.

Richard DeVos is in Green's camp. When I asked him about the single most critical piece of advice he would give to his grandchildren or any ambitious young person, DeVos didn't hesitate: "Start your own business and keep it private." That's the advice he says he gave his own grandson and namesake. Young Rick

DeVos started Spout.com to bring films from around the world that have not experienced theatrical distribution directly to a movie lover's computer. Thanks to his grandfather's influence and wise counsel, Rick DeVos, in his twenties, is an entrepreneur attempting to bust open a closed Hollywood system and let consumers—not the Hollywood studios—decide what movies they wish to see and when.

Savannah's success story, Bob Jepson, has enjoyed three wealth-creation successes: Jepson Corporation, Kuhlman, and Coburn Optical Industries. But before he was making all the big decisions himself, he worked for other companies and found it frustrating when he was told by one early boss, "Bob, you want to move faster than the institution is willing to move." Looking back now, he admits that it was a great education on someone else's dime, but he knew deep in his heart that he was an entrepreneur. He says, "I loved working with people, but I liked working with people better than *for* people."

Burlington, Vermont's Robert P. Stiller likes working with people, too, but he only really understands working for himself because that is all he's ever done. In 1981, after the sale of his previous company, EZ Wider (one guess as to what his favorite movie was at the time), he stumbled onto or tipped his cup in the direction of his next big idea while vacationing in Vermont. That morning, Stiller enjoyed the first cup of what he thought was the best coffee he'd ever had. Even though he wasn't much of a coffee drinker, he was driven to track down the roaster of the particular coffee beans that he so enjoyed. He found what would be the source of his wealth in a local Waitsfield, Vermont, firm called Green Mountain Coffee Roasters. Stiller thought: "If I like this cup of joe, then there may be a great market among real coffee lovers for a higher-quality premium coffee." He bought the small roasting company, hired himself again, and started the super-premium coffee revolution.

It wasn't an instant success, however. Green Mountain bled

red for the first four years. "No one ever said the entrepreneurial life is an easy life, but it sure is an exciting one," he says. I'm not certain it was so exciting when he had exhausted the entire fortune he'd derived from his EZ Wider success in his attempt to build Green Mountain to greatness. He doesn't remember the pain today as much as he celebrates that Green Mountain is the most successful super-premium coffee company in the country. Looking back, Stiller says, "It was all about survival." A decade later, the coffee was roasting and the company was cooking. He took Green Mountain public in 1993, further enriching the firm and fueling the company's expansion. That move expanded Stiller's wallet as well. Today Vermont's most successful man is outfitting his yacht so he can spend a few more weeks a year on the high seas. He says he learned his success and wealth-creation philosophy from his father, who always said, "If you provide the best product or service and treat people well, you will be successful at whatever you do." He clearly had a good idea in super-premium coffee; he focused maniacally on the manufacturing aspect—the roasting process; and he pursued the building of the company with his characteristic passion. Stiller's love of life and continual pursuit of greater meaning through his meditation and his enjoyment of what he calls "the amenities of life" (boats, planes, art) prove that he has not only survived, but thrived.

What DeVos, Hartzler, Mathile, Jepson, Stiller, and virtually all RMITs have done in their illustrious careers is to write their own personal declarations of independence. According to the Federal Reserve Board, in 2007, *the average net worth of self-employed people was an impressive $1.3 million, more than six times the net worth of the average worker.*

Jim Oelschlager, the ace card player of Akron, Ohio, mustered the courage to write his declaration of independence. He left the comfort of a cushy job at Firestone Tire to start his own company, Oak Associates, Ltd. Today it's one of the leading investment management companies in the country in performance.

Oelschlager is often hailed by *Forbes*, *Fortune*, *Worth*, and *Money* magazines as one of the best investment managers of all time. His personal investment and his investment skills have yielded prodigious profits for his investors and himself. With $30 billion of assets under management and a personal net worth of hundreds of millions, Oelschlager is an inspiration in countless ways. As noted earlier, perhaps most impressive is that he had the guts to build his own company even after being diagnosed with multiple sclerosis, knowing full well that he could soon be bound to a wheelchair for the rest of his life. He has refused to permit his physical limitations to become life limitations. With characteristic humility, he says, "There are no extraordinary people—there are only average people who do extraordinary things." The owner of Oak Associates is referred to by his associates (he calls them Oakies) as the "benevolent dictator." He says, "Democracy works well in government, but not in businesses. Consensus management doesn't work." He likes picking winning stocks for his clients—and yes, he likes running his own show and being his own boss.

Wichita, Kansas's Phil Ruffin, a multibillionaire real estate developer, oil tycoon, hotel owner, and manufacturer, exclaims: "I could never work for someone else. You don't get rich working for other people!" Ruffin finished only three years of college, then dropped out to flip burgers before starting to build what ultimately became the Ruffin Companies. Today he owns diverse real estate interests, including the Trump International Hotel and Tower; the Frontier Hotel and Casino in Las Vegas; the Wichita Greyhound Racing Park; Harper Hand Trucks, the largest hand truck company in the world; sixty-one Total convenience stores; and a hundred oil wells. All of his companies are 100 percent owned by Ruffin. He developed the Crystal Palace Casino in the Bahamas and sold it for $147 million in 2005. His coup de grâce, however, was his sale of thirty-four acres of prime land directly on the Las Vegas Strip for a stunning $41 million an acre, reaping an even more stunning total of $1.4 billion. Now, he says, "I'm buying a billion dollars' worth of bonds a day." Plus, he kept seven acres on the Las Vegas Strip for his own development. Three and a half of those acres currently house his joint venture with best buddy Donald Trump, the Trump International Hotel and Tower. Ruffin is proud that he has never invested in any publicly traded stocks, instead choosing to invest solely in his own businesses. He says, "Why would I invest in some other company where the management is sucking it dry in salary and stock options? I'll stick to my own things."

In 1973, Lake Charles, Louisiana's captain courageous William J. Doré traded his 49 percent stake in a company called Ebbco—with revenues of $1.5 million—for ownership of 100 percent of Global Divers, a company on the brink of bankruptcy. His family, friends, and even the seller thought he was insane. Why did he do it? Doré says, "I only owned 49 percent of the business I was supposedly running and I didn't have control over the business decisions." His new company sounded impressive, but Global Divers was anything but global at the time. The offshore diving company would soon live up to its grand name, however, thanks to Doré's strong belief in his abilities as an entrepreneur totally responsible for the success or failure of his enterprise. Today Global Industries Ltd. has a market capitalization of $2 billion and Doré has a treasure chest with more than $700 million.

Bruce Halle of Scottsdale, Arizona, and Discount Tire dynamo, clearly loves owning his own business—he has for forty-eight years. But he also believes that the people you choose to accompany you on the journey are critical to your success. He asks the rhetorical question, "How the hell did we get here after all these years?" He answers himself: "By a lot of hard work, with the help of some terrific people, and with a simple but powerful business philosophy." Halle's philosophy? "Be fair, be truthful, work hard, be there on time, and help people." Helping people has helped Halle build one heck of a company that he says even more than forty years later is still the best reason to wake up in the morning. "There is nothing more fulfilling than owning your own business and seeing that business create jobs for good people and value for good customers."

Harris Rosen, the richest man in Orlando, Florida, had the guts to leave the comfort of corporate America (Disney Resorts) when he bought his first hotel in 1974 at age thirty. He says, "My life really began once I owned my first hotel—there is nothing like the pride of ownership. It's a uniquely American sensibility, and I say God bless America for it."

Bear in mind that for most people, the need for security is a major impediment to becoming super-wealthy. If the stability of a steady salary is critical to you, then please understand that you'll likely never become the richest man or woman in town. Working for the other man too long makes you risk-averse, and the ability to take responsible risk is what often distinguishes an RMIT from an also-ran. Be the man (or woman), not an also-ran.

Salt Lake City's Jon Huntsman has always been the man, and a smart risk taker, too. In his book *Winners Never Cheat: Everyday Values We Learned as Children (But May Have Forgotten)*, he says, "Most people don't take personal risks and will never know the true joy and satisfaction that comes from the mine-filled arenas where great empires are built." A graph of the life of a typical RMIT would look a lot like an electrocardiogram. Huntsman's journey certainly would. He grew up very poor as the son of a rural schoolteacher whom he describes as a "harsh disciplinarian." He remembers only one 50-cent piece that his father gave him during his entire life. He made his own money and his own way from a very early age, once personally paying $120 to the dentist to rid him of a mouthful of cavities when he was in the eighth grade. He says, "I always felt trapped in my personal situation." He moved with his family from a small two-room house in backwoods Blackfoot, Idaho, to a one-bedroom apartment for five people before ultimately spending his high school years in a cramped Quonset hut in student housing at Stanford University, where his father was pursuing a PhD in education. The move to Palo Alto meant an even more meager existence, but it did have one advantage. It led Huntsman to Palo Alto High School, where he became the student body president and the big man on campus. His performance at Palo Alto High and his drive won him a scholarship to the Wharton School. He knew from experience, however, that he did not want to live the kind of lifestyle his father had favored. He hasn't lived a meager life since, by any means. Still, Huntsman's career and life have not been straight lines to success. His company was on the verge of bankruptcy twice, and he's defeated cancer three times.

In each case, he worked through the tough times by relying on his confidence in his abilities, his Mormon faith, and his moral compass. Like Huntsman, RMITs are not afraid of risk. While they certainly are not comfortable with irresponsible risk, they are comfortable with volatility. They know how to ride the roller coaster of life, preparing for the peaks and valleys of building their businesses, cultivating their fortunes, and creating exciting lives. They love the ride, no matter how bumpy it becomes.

Typical of this RMIT ability to manage volatility, Dennis Albaugh, the Iowa farm boy once dubbed the Pesticide Prince by *Forbes* magazine, says he mortgaged his home in order to purchase a truck that he filled with weed killer to sell to a potential customer. Alas, his prized new possession leaked all the way from Iowa to South Dakota, leaving him with nothing to sell and no money in his pocket. Most people would have called that a sign from God. But Dennis Albaugh simply rented another truck, bought more weed killer, this time on credit, and barely broke even. However, his business was born. "The single thing that most affected my success was my ability to be a risk taker and to have the courage to start my own business," he says. "Mind you, there was never any clear-cut path or proof that my ideas were going to work." His ideas have worked, all right: Starting with that one truckload of pesticides in 1979, he built Albaugh, Inc., into one of the world's leading agricultural chemicals companies. The owner of the largest supplier of off-patent weed-killing chemicals in the world, who is now worth billions, says, "I really like working for me."

Jim Harrison, Tuscaloosa's RMIT, loved taking one small family pharmacy and building a company that encompassed over 150 drugstores in the Southeast. In 1997, virtually every major national pharmacy chain competed to buy Harrison's Harco. Rite Aid ultimately won the prize. Harrison says, "There is no greater pleasure than owning your own business. I love the pace, I love the competition, I love the responsibility. I never considered working for the other guy. And to this day, my former employees call me and say they long for the days of Camelot."

Milwaukee's main man, William Kellogg (no relation to the cereal fortune), started as an assistant store manager with Kohl's, the Wisconsin-based retail chain, in 1967 and is the rare RMIT who worked his way up the corporate food chain. He became the chairman and chief executive officer in 1977. Then in 1986, he switched from being a highly respected and generously compensated CEO to an owner when he led the management team and a group of investors in buying Kohl's from then-owner British American Tobacco Company. Kellogg took the department store public in 1992 for a big personal payday. A couple of billion dollars in his coffers later, Kellogg, who never went to college, says, "Kohl's was my life, and I have loved my life. There is nothing so sweet as having a piece of the action while doing what you love most."

The Partner Paradox

That piece of action is rarely, if ever, achieved without the counsel, expertise, and support of trustworthy partners. Becoming the richest man in town requires both cunning and collaboration. In other words, none of us is as smart as all of us. In business and in your life, great success is hard to achieve without help from other people, on many fronts. None of us can do it all, no matter how brilliant we think we might be. That doesn't mean there has to be equal ownership, however. *RMITs all say that one critical key to creating great wealth is to hold all the cards.*

Jim Oelschlager of Akron formed Oak Associates with the following terms: Don't have a partner. Use your own money. Don't buy out another business. Don't sell out to another company. Dennis Albaugh of Des Moines, Iowa, feels even more strongly: "I hate partners. Every time I have had partners, I have found that I have spent my time trying to figure out how to get out of the partnership. I've never considered going public because then you're not in control. I do like banks as partners, though. The nice thing about banks is, once you pay them off, they go away." Albaugh tells the story of how he once got a loan for some much-needed mezzanine financing by pledging 2 percent of the company. "One of the happiest days of my life was when we paid off that loan. My employees had a bonfire to burn the loan documents." Nevertheless, he says, "While I have never liked the idea of partners, I have always hired people who are smarter than I am." I heard this refrain from virtually every RMIT I interviewed. One hundred percent of RMITs agree that selecting the right team, the right employees, and the best advisers has been essential to their individual success and ultimate wealth creation. No one goes it alone; we live in an interdependent world—but make no mistake: *Sole or majority ownership is the key to becoming the richest man in town.*

Dan Duncan, Houston's humble billionaire, quotes the Bible (Proverbs 13:20) when he posits, "He who walks with wise men shall be wise." RMITs warn that you must make certain you choose wise colleagues possessed of impeccable integrity to be a part of your enterprise. RMITs know that a reckless, narcissistic, or self-indulgent partner can ruin an enterprise overnight.

Some rare RMITs, however, got really lucky in choosing a partner. Fred DeLuca, the founder of Subway, has had the same perfect partner for more than forty years. Dr. Peter Buck gave DeLuca a $1,000 capital infusion and, perhaps more important, the suggestion and encouragement to start a submarine sandwich shop as a way of paying for Fred's college education. The key to this great partnership is that Buck stood back and watched with pride as DeLuca built Subway into the multibillion-dollar business it is today. Buck's brilliance was recognizing that there couldn't be two kings. Today DeLuca presides over more than twenty-nine thousand Subway stores, making both Buck and DeLuca billionaires. Buck chose the right horse to bet on, and then he let that thoroughbred win the race.

This is not to say that an equal partnership is impossible. Jorge Pérez of Miami has a partner in The Related Group, Stephen Ross, whom he met as a student at the University of Michigan. The two couldn't be more different in style: Ross is the hard-charging native New Yorker; Pérez, the son of Cuban exiles who grew up in Argentina and Colombia, exudes Latin charm and charisma. Their complementary strengths are one reason the business marriage has worked so lucratively. Ross runs The Related Group in New York, and Jorge manages the Miami company—having well-defined separate fiefdoms may be another explanation for their successful partnership. Still, Pérez says, "Steve is my best friend and my mentor." Together they have built a company that is one of the nation's largest builders of multifamily housing.

Whether picking a partner or hiring a staff, there's more to look for than just general smarts and integrity. For some ambitious RMITs, collaborating is the only way to move ahead as fast as they almost always want to travel. William Sanders of El Paso advises, "Choose team players who share your values and passions, but also ones who have complementary skills. There are people who are good at managing process, at deploying capital, selling, or being strategic thinkers, but I have yet to find someone who is outstanding at all of these." Albany's Guha Bala adds, "If you must partner, always partner with someone smarter than you are." I guess this means he considers his brother Karthik Bala the smart one: Guha Bala clearly respects and values his brother's intellect and skills, but he also possesses a good measure of humility. RMITs prize humility, which might sound surprising given their monumental achievements.

When I asked California's Red Emmerson when he first realized that he was the richest man in his town, the billionaire timber baron and real estate developer replied, "Probably long after when I was." Humility does not preclude a healthy ego—*healthy* being the operative word here. A healthy ego assures confidence, ambition, and resilience in the face of adversity. "Arrogance, however, will ultimately bite you in the ass," says Emmerson. His humility, perhaps, is the reason he has been the boss of Sierra Pacific Industries for more than sixty years and still retains the deep loyalty of his best people. Bernard Marcus of Home Depot fame has loads of confidence, but plenty of humility, too, when he says, "Arthur Blank and I together created a company with 120,000 employees and a market capitalization in excess of $100 billion when I stepped down. Arthur and I couldn't have done it without the dedication of all Home Depot employees." His Home Depot home run allowed him to set up the Marcus Family Foundation, through which he built Atlanta's Georgia Aquarium at the cost of a reported $200 million donation. He also set up the Marcus Institute to help children with neurological disabilities. This largesse is just a drop in the ocean of philanthropic work that Marcus is now passionately pursuing. This ability to make such a difference in the lives of others is one of the greatest rewards of being an RMIT. It would have been impossible to realize had Marcus not found a great partner in Arthur Blank—and had he not had the humility to know how critical a good partner, not to mention 120,000 dedicated employees, was to ensuring his success.

According to Jim Oelschlager of Akron, Ohio, the secret to happiness is "Get a good partner and have a good partnership." You'll remember Oelschlager, the same RMIT who started his company with four rules, one of which was to hold all the cards. His definition of partnership, however, is more complex than what we usually think of as a fifty–fifty relationship. As a benevolent dictator, Oelschlager's idea of a successful partnership certainly means sharing the wealth, but it does not mean sharing the ownership control. He knows how to pick great partners, though—his key team has been with him for more than thirty years.

Hartley Peavey, the Mississippi music man whose company bears his name, is the oldest son of a Meridian music store owner. He doesn't call himself a benevolent dictator—though he clearly is; instead he calls himself a catalyst. "I learned in high school chemistry class that the definition of *catalyst* is 'that which enhances or speeds up a reaction without itself being changed.' I am the guy who is always stirring up the pot, demanding new ideas, new approaches, new products," he says. But he claims he is still the same guy he was when he started his company more than forty years ago. "I will not let anybody call me Mr. Peavey," he says. He may not have changed with all his wealth and success, but he asserted to me that he has gotten much smarter. "I thought when I graduated from college that I knew something. I didn't realize that a diploma is nothing but a learner's permit," says Peavey.

Alex Hartzler of Harrisburg, Pennsylvania, serves up an ace when he says, "Just as a good tennis player never gets better unless he plays with players better than he is, the surest way to outsize success is to surround yourself with people who are smarter, faster, and better than you. That's how you sharpen

your game. That's how you become the best player in your field."
During the growth of Webclients, he recognized the strengths
of his partners Josh Gray and Scott Piotroski, and even though
it meant taking a less prominent role at times, he knew he was
surrounded by partners who brought mission-critical skills to
the organization. Together they built and ultimately sold Webclients to ValueClick for $141 million. It was a very prominent
payday for all.

RMITs know their perfect pitch and deploy their unique skills
in businesses they can control or have a major role in shaping.
But they also know that finding the right partner or partners,
with complementary skills, is critical to success in any venture
or enterprise. If you are the visionary, make darn certain you
have a partner who is a financial and operational genius. Know
thyself, know thy strengths and weaknesses, and find thy ace
partner. But if possible, hold all the ace cards: BYOB.

- Be the man (or woman); don't work for the man (or
  woman).
- Find the founder in you—94 percent of RMITs founded
  their own companies.
- Be a benevolent dictator—share the wealth, but keep the
  ownership.
- Partner only with those who bring something mission-
  critical to your success.

RMIT Commandment #4

GET ADDICTED TO AMBITION

If we did all the things we are capable of doing, we would literally astound ourselves.

—Thomas Edison

Now that you know who you are, having analyzed your own unique talents and innate interests, and now that you're convinced the surest way to become the richest man in town is to own your own business, you are ready to crank up the volume of your ambition. All the self-discovery in the world is useless if you don't have the desire and the will to become the richest man or woman in town. There is also no denying the crucial role that hard work, dedication, and diligence play in reaching the American Dream. In other words, there is no wealth without ambition. Much effort equals much prosperity.

New York's most ambitious man, Carl Icahn, believes a healthy obsession builds a wealthy bank account. Icahn is often referred to as America's unlocker of inherent corporate value. This activist investor—who is also perhaps the most feared man in business (just ask Time Warner's Dick Parsons or Yahoo!'s Jerry Yang)—says, "You have to be obsessive to be successful."

He loves what he does every day and can't imagine doing anything different: "If you find something you enjoy doing, then your work is not work." Convenience store and casino king Phil Ruffin of Wichita admonishes, "You've got to work hard; you've got to love to work; and you've got to have fun doing it. You can't sit around and go to the beach. You've got to have high-octane ambition." He does: In the early days of building his Total convenience store business, he notes, "I was traveling to three cities a day. It was hard, it was tiring, but I knew it was worth it."

Parents Matter

The level of ambition of RMIT parents seems to have had a powerful effect on the way in which many RMITs developed their personal ambition. Phil Ruffin has the same work ethic and ambition now—while buying $1 billion worth of bonds a day—as he did when he was first building his fortune. He says, "My father owned a grocery business—and all he did was work, and he was happy. I learned early that hard work makes you happy."

Anderson, California's Red Emmerson says, "My father didn't have much ambition. He wanted to make just enough money to exist. I had much greater ambitions. Maybe it was because I was born in 1929. I knew I was poor and I knew I didn't want to be that way in the future."

Carl Icahn's father was a struggling musician who seemed, at least to Carl, to accept his station in life. Carl had bigger plans. "As middle-class Jews, my parents were basically socialist, and I had a problem with that philosophy because with socialism there is no incentive. In politics or in business there must be incentive and accountability." This early realization has formed the basis for Icahn's approach to business. He believes that many Fortune 500 companies are run like socialist systems, and as a result he is determined to change the way corporations are governed. He's currently blogging about it in his Icahn Report, which is designed to keep corporate CEOs on their toes.

William D. Sanders of El Paso, whose dad was a respected advertising agency owner, says, "My father was known for his skills and was indeed highly respected, but he was never able to turn that respect into capital—personal wealth. I always wanted both—respect and wealth. I never saw them as contradictory in any way." Colorado Springs real estate developer Leroy Landhuis—who grew up on the farm outside a town of two hundred people—says, "My parents simply accepted their lot in life. We never left the farm except to go to church. I knew there was more and I wanted more for myself than my parents wanted for me." Seeking a better life is a powerful motivator, no doubt, but the good news about ambition is that it can be honed.

You can't acquire new talents, but you can kick-start your ambition addiction, you can turn up the volume of your work ethic, you can be more persistent, and you can cultivate a sense of fearlessness. You can and must be the creative force in your own life—taking personal responsibility for your success and understanding that you have the power to achieve it.

Get Hooked

Psychologists tell us that we are all addicted to something—often to many things. The very essence of our humanness is, in fact, often defined by our personal addictions. The list of American addictions is seemingly endless: coffee, exercise, sex, cigarettes, chocolate, junk food, drugs, alcohol, love, admiration, fame, reality TV, eBay, Facebook, mail-order catalogs, online shopping, and, yes, success. You can decide which are the good addictions, the life-affirming ones versus the life-debilitating ones. But why not replace those bad addictions with good ones? RMITs do. They love to work—although, curiously, they rarely describe themselves as workaholics (New York's Carl Icahn does, however). These qualities of persistence, diligence, work ethic, and self-belief are not genetic traits that are doled out to only a few truly gifted people. These are equal-opportunity addictions. We all have the ability to become addicted to the traits that help us seize success and create wealth. Hard work and self-belief are habits that each of us can develop and hone to a fine brilliance. Aristotle once observed: "We are what we repeatedly do. Excellence, then, is not an act, but a habit."

Writing is a good addiction. So is thinking through problems and developing solutions, even improving things that already work well. RMITs are often innovation junkies who refuse to settle for merely good enough. In terms of becoming an RMIT, working hard is perhaps the best addiction you can have. David Rubenstein, Washington, DC's private equity powerhouse, believes in hard work and persistence. He doesn't believe in what he thinks is one of the most overused words in the English language—*genius*. The former Carter White House aide and CEO of the Carlyle Group was described to me by some of his colleagues as a genius. He doesn't buy it. He says, "When you get older in life, you realize there are very few geniuses in this world. Most likely, you will never meet one, and Randy, you did not meet one today."

Growing up poor in 1950s Baltimore, Maryland, instilled in Rubenstein a keen sense of ambition. In our interview, he seemed to anticipate my every question and launch into the answer seemingly before I could ask it. He is one of the most intelligent men I met on my RMIT expedition, and yet he does not credit his intelligence for his success. Rather, he says, "The reason some people get farther ahead of other people is because they possess persistence." He defines persistence as the ability to refuse to take no for an answer.

Rubenstein remembers that his life changed dramatically on November 4, 1980, when his boss at the time, President Jimmy Carter, was soundly defeated by Ronald Reagan. He also recalls how many people in the legal, political, and business circles he frequented while in his White House power seat complimented him on his intelligence and professionalism. Many of the Washington elite told him that if he ever needed a job, he should give them a call. "Ronald Reagan became president and I called those very same people who thought I was so smart, and you know what? They did not return my calls," he says. He could have joined a local law firm, of course, but while he had been learning the ropes of politics, his law school classmates had been learning to be good lawyers. He would have been significantly behind the curve of his peer group. He didn't want to be a lawyer anyway— that was not his perfect pitch. Rubenstein decided he wanted to start an investment company of his own, one that succeeded or failed based on his ambition, diligence, and determination. He wanted to control his future. Like all RMITs, he was tired of working for someone else, even if that someone else happened to be the president of the United States.

Rubenstein's persistence paid off. As he was raising money to start his first investment fund, he says, "One investor said to me nine times in a row, 'I don't think your fund is right for me.' But I kept going back and on the tenth time, he said, 'Okay, here's some money.' He became our largest investor over time." Rubenstein knew what he wanted, and his persistence and his ambition allowed him to get it.

O. Bruton Smith, the richest man in Charlotte, North Carolina, says, "Persistence is the mother's milk of success." The person he most admires is Ross Perot, one of the most successful men in Dallas, Texas, and certainly the most successful person that Texarkana has ever produced. "Ross started at the bottom and he didn't stop until he reached the top," Smith says. "Whether it was running EDS, Perot Systems, or running for president, Ross is always full-throttle." Smith, the founder and chairman of NASCAR track owner Speedway Motorsports, Inc., and chairman of Sonic Automotive, knows a thing or two about full-throttle ambition, hard work, perseverance, and what he calls "essential energy." He started out life as a North Carolina farm boy and today is a multibillionaire known in racing circles as the man who took NASCAR to Wall Street. Add to that the ownership of 168 automobile dealerships and control of thirty-four collision-repair centers. He notes: "The ladder of opportunity is rather tall. I am always trying to get to the top, but it is a never-ending ladder." To most mere mortals, Bruton Smith has long been perched on the top rung, but in his early eighties, his ambition is not yet sated, nor has his work ethic waned. "From the time I had a tricycle, I wanted a bicycle, and from the time I had one car, I wanted another one, and I have never run out of energy."

Smith and Rubenstein would no doubt agree with Calvin Coolidge when he posited that "nothing in this world can take the place of persistence. Talent will not; nothing is more common than unsuccessful people with talent. Genius will not; unrewarded genius is almost a proverb. Education will not; the world is full of educated derelicts. Persistence and determination alone are omnipotent. The slogan 'press on' has solved and always will solve the problems of the human race." Ambition requires Coolidge's press-on mentality. It also demands constant care and feeding.

Ambition Attention

Bob Stiller, the rich roaster of rich coffees at Green Mountain Coffee in Vermont, has been one to press on indefatigably from the time he was adopted by his parents at birth, it seems. He is also a born salesman—making a pitch is his perfect pitch. He admits, though, that being an adopted child might have something to do with his strong desire to prove himself continually. He says, "I've just begun to understand the psychological impact of my formative years." Even so, he took careful note of his father's work ethic and independence as the owner of his own heating coil business. He also developed an early interest in the power of visualizing what he wanted out of life. One of the things he visualized was a shiny red Corvette. He cut out a picture of his dream and carefully taped it to the lamp in his room. As the biggest success story in Burlington, Vermont—indeed, the richest man in Vermont—he did ultimately get that visualized Corvette, though he much prefers his Jaguar XKE (his actual first sports car) and his Ferrari. Stiller has gotten considerably more than he visualized, but he still uses the power of visualization in his company and in his personal life today. "I still cut out pictures of what I want the company to achieve," he says, "and the amazing thing is, the things that I have visualized have come to me."

Stiller's ambition is high-octane and highly caffeinated, no doubt, but it is packaged in a Vermont teddy bear persona. Nevertheless, he's very much addicted to a daily cup of ambition: Howard Schultz's Starbucks may still be on every street corner, but it is not the star of the coffee industry—Green Mountain is. With a market capitalization nearing the billion-dollar mark, Green Mountain has, in terms of profits, become the most financially successful premium coffee company in the country over the past decade. Stiller's ambition led him to his company's success and to what he calls "the amenities in life," which he has attained—jets, a yacht, and a world-class art collection. He says, "Success is the ability to achieve the things you want in life." But even though he has achieved the things he wants in life, he is still climbing—every day. He says, "We all have within ourselves the capability to accentuate our ambition and we all have the ability to choose to be diligent workers—to be doers." He gives much of the credit for his successful thinking to a Silva meditation and mind-development course that he says changed his whole perspective on the world. "People don't realize the power we have in our minds," says Stiller. Destiny to him is not a matter of chance, but rather a matter of choice. *Your destiny is in direct proportion to your ambition addiction.*

When I asked Roxanne Quimby of Portland, Maine, what was the single best piece of advice she would give an ambitious young person looking for the success she has enjoyed, she replied, "It sounds trite, but I know it to be true: Hard work is the only sure path to success. It simply can't be avoided. Nor should it be, because work should be enjoyable." Jim Oelschlager reminds us of Colin Powell's wise words—"All work is honorable." To RMITs, work is not a four-letter word. On the contrary: Because they love what they do, because they have found their perfect pitch, work is simply what they do to get things accomplished, which in turn leads to that great by-product of ambitious achievement—financial success.

Fargo, North Dakota's Gary Tharaldson earned very little cold hard cash on his first job as a farmworker—only $1.25 an hour. His father worked on the same farm and made a whopping $1.75 an hour. Yet Tharaldson's father brought up six kids on that meager salary. It's no surprise, then, that Tharaldson has never been afraid of work. He loves working. Even more, he loves outworking everybody else. He says, "Whether I was selling insurance or building hotels, I have always outworked the next guy, happily." It is clear from interviewing these RMITs that there are varying definitions of ambition among the manifestly motivated. They all, however, agree on one thing: Work is inevitable, and it is fun—so much fun that the average RMIT happily puts in more than sixty hours per week. Miami's Jorge Pérez proudly admits to working eighteen-hour days. "I so love doing what I do that I can't think of anything to which I would rather be devoting my time," he says. "My work life, family life, and social lives are all intertwined—they're seamless."

Pérez's neighbor to the north in Fort Lauderdale, Florida, Wayne Huizenga, is one of the great serial entrepreneurs in American history, with a net worth in excess of $3 billion. He says, "I was always the first one in the office and the last one to leave." At a celebration after the sale of Blockbuster Video, as war stories were being traded, he learned that many of his colleagues had enjoyed a secret game where they took turns trying to beat him to the office. "I learned that one morning a colleague, Bob Garren, arrived at the office at 5:00 a.m. determined to beat me, but I had arrived at 4:30. It wasn't a competitive thing for me. It's just that every day, I couldn't wait to get to work, because I enjoyed it so much. I wanted to be there all the time." Huizenga's ambition addiction and work ethic led to the joke circulating through the halls of Blockbuster: "If you don't show up on Saturday, don't bother coming in on Sunday." Huizenga's talent is the ability to spot companies that can dominate an industry.

Along his golden-paved journey, he spotted many. He bought and built a bottled water company, a pest control company, a chain of dry cleaners, and a uniform rentals company. As America's ace of acquisitions, Huizenga offers his personal business success secret when he says, "I don't buy companies, I buy industries. That's why I got into the automobile business forming AutoNation—because the automobile industry is a trillion-dollar industry, and a small piece of a big pie is very tasty." His Midas touch certainly continued with AutoNation, which went from a simple concept with zero revenue to $20 billion of sales in two years, making it the largest automobile dealership company in the country with 375 dealerships. Hard work and healthy ambition have served Huizenga well.

But bear in mind that hard work for hard work's sake is not the point. Boston's Pete Nicholas, the co-founder and chairman of Boston Scientific, the $20 billion medical devices company, points out that ambition has its limitations. "Generic ambition without a sense of purpose will not take you very far," he warns. "You've got to have conviction around a single idea that you believe in so intently, you can't envision anything but greatness coming from it. Then you've got to be willing to work hard to make that idea become a reality." Jim Oelschlager also knows the importance of having a sense of purpose. He cautions us not to mistake activity for accomplishment when he says, "Don't confuse mere motion with progress." Meridian, Mississippi's

Hartley Peavey places focus at the top of his list of traits critical to success: Without focus, you waste your energy. In his slow Southern drawl, his quick, highly focused mind says, "If you chase two rabbits, both will escape."

For RMITs, work is both honorable and fun, so why do so many of us hate the thought of hard work? Hartley Peavey, using a common RMIT pilot's analogy, says, "Most people fly in ground effect. They operate at the minimum level of acceptance, which means that point in their work effort where they are doing just enough not to get fired or just enough to get by. But they aren't willing to flap their wings to fly above ground effect. I spend a lot of my time encouraging the people of Peavey to rise to their greatest level, to dare to be different. Maybe 3 percent of the people get the message and internalize it. The others are just warming the chairs."

Many RMITs believe that fear of failure is often the reason for this just-warming-the-chairs affliction. Sheldon Adelson—once worth over $28 billion and the richest man in Las Vegas—has said to anyone willing to listen, "If you are afraid of losing, you will never succeed." This fearlessness requires supreme self-confidence, something RMITs possess in spades. They believe in themselves and they believe in investing in themselves. Adelson, who grew up on the wrong side of the tracks as the son of a taxi driver in Boston, says, "If you don't have a conviction about what you are doing, you are never going to make it." And what conviction he must possess. Recently, his personal fortune has been deflated by over $20 billion. Adelson's Las Vegas Sands Corporation, which owns the Venetian Hotel and Casino in Las Vegas and the Venetian Casino in Macau, the former Portuguese colony near the coast of China, lost more than 90 percent of its value in one year. He and many other casino moguls believed fervently that Macau would become the hottest hotel and casino location in the world, but Chinese leaders believed differently and curtailed mass-market visas to visit the black jack tables of Macau.

Although it remains to be seen whether Macau will become the next gambling mecca and salvage Adelson's fortune, for now, he seems characteristically stoic. Perhaps because of his track-record or his supreme confidence, he hasn't lost his conviction. He is still not afraid to fail. Before Adelson became the RMIT in Vegas, he owned COMDEX, the first computer dealers' trade show, which he sold to Japanese investment company Softbank in 1995 for $862 million. Not only is he fearless, he knows when to exit a business—COMDEX no longer exists. When opening the fifty-story Palazzo Resort Hotel and Casino on the Vegas Strip, Adelson boasted to *USA Today* regarding his competitors, "We will cannibalize them."

With statements like that, making friends as a means of influencing people is clearly not what Adelson is all about. And his highly debited checkbook proves the point. This may be an example of what Pete Nicholas of Boston calls "ambition without a conscience," the dark side of ambition, and that is not what he or most RMITs strive for. Rather, they strive to be the best they can possibly be, to harness their ambition to a good purpose. Ambition addiction comes with the side effect of supreme self-confidence, but ambition without a purpose can lead to an overdose. There is a difference. The former is the belief you can succeed; arrogance is the belief you can't fail.

Gary Tharaldson of Fargo, North Dakota, shows a healthy self-confidence when he says, "If I had to do it all over again, I know I could." Believing you can is the crucial first step to any success, let alone a billion-dollar bank account. He adds, "The height of your success will be proportionate to the depth of your self-belief." Jon Huntsman of Salt Lake City agrees, saying, "You must believe you can succeed or by definition you have failed." When I asked Fred Levin of Pensacola who he considered the smartest person he ever met and what he had learned from him or her, he said, "Good question . . . hmmm . . . I have never known anyone who thinks as logically as I do." That's the confidence and self-belief of an RMIT. After a few beats, he offered up his law partner, Martin Proctor, as one of the most "effective" people he has ever known because of his outstanding organizational skills—skills that Levin covets highly. Levin's response to this question was not unique. Pete Nicholas said, "There has been no Disraeli-like figure in my life, though many people have touched and influenced me in many ways." *Most RMITs had a hard time answering the question of who is the smartest person they know because, let's face it, they are that person.*

Thirty-something Philadelphia boy wonder, technology guru, and venture capitalist Josh Kopelman is one smart RMIT—no doubt the smartest guy he knows, though he would never admit it. He would admit, however, that he knows how to spot a good opportunity, and that he knows a thing or two about good ambition addiction. He sold his company Half.com to eBay in 2000 for $355 million, at the age of twenty-nine. "I'm hoping to step up to the plate dozens of times in my lifetime," he says, "and I'm hoping that my lifetime batting average is high—that's what it's all about. There is always a next rung on the ladder of success."

But as you climb those rungs of success, Chicago's Sam Zell says, the real secret to success is what he calls his eleventh commandment: "Thou shalt not take oneself too seriously." Even so, Zell is described by most who know him as audaciously ambitious, but he simply calls himself a "professional opportunist." He recently availed himself of the opportunity to attempt a much-needed turnaround of the 165-year-old Tribune Company, the media conglomerate that owns the *Chicago Tribune*, the *Los Angeles Times*, the *Baltimore Sun*, the Chicago Cubs, and twenty-three TV stations. Often a contrarian, he still believes that old media like newspapers have some life left in them in the Internet age. When asked what his greatest achievement is, he says, "I don't ever respond in terms of epiphanies or greatest achievements because I'm still achieving. One day, I'll be judged by the body of my work, but right now I'm still working!"

"Still working" also characterizes Wayne Huizenga, Fort Lauderdale's colorful billionaire. At seventy, he continues to have the keen ambition and desire to spot new opportunities. Even with the successes of Waste Management, Blockbuster, Auto-Nation, Extended Stay America, and enough other companies to stretch to the sports stadium he owns in Miami, Huizenga is always thinking about the next wealth-creation opportunity. When asked what the future holds for his old company, Blockbuster, in this digital age, he says, "I don't own the stock now." While he may not be bullish on the company as it currently exists under New York RMIT Carl Icahn's auspices, Huizenga can't help but ponder another possible future for his old home. "Blockbuster has fifty-five hundred stores, and if you and I could figure out what to do with them, we could create the next great American business," he muses. "We could acquire the company for half a billion dollars, and if we could put the right things in those fifty-five hundred stores, we could hit a huge home run. Blockbuster's real estate is either a huge opportunity or a huge liability, but if we could turn those fifty-five hundred stores into something else that the public really needs, we could create another multi-billion-dollar company." Like the typical RMIT that he is, he never stops thinking, searching, or questing. He is as ambitious today as he was when he started out hauling trash for a living.

Bob "Mr. Alaska" Gillam, like Huizenga, never stops thinking about the future—and like Sam Zell he never takes himself too seriously. He says, "I employ a sense of fun and adventure in everything I do." He is as ambitious in his extracurricular activities as he is in managing money. That sense of adventure leads him to fly airplanes, go snow skiing, and invest billions of dollars around the world through his investment company, McKinley Capital Management. He says, "In the early '90s when I started McKinley Capital, people thought I was mad to start a money management firm in Alaska, but my ambition drove me to prove them wrong." That ambition allowed him to jump some big hurdles, not the least of which was his remote location; at that time, Anchorage was not a major communications center. "We couldn't afford T-1 lines," Gillam says, "so we were one of the first investment firms to use satellite for data transfer." RMITs find solutions to often-vexing obstacles because their ambition and confidence allow them to take on what might seem like insurmountable problems to the less ambitiously addicted.

"Solving the seemingly unsolvable is what I do best—it is what turns me on most," says Philadelphia's Josh Kopelman. Gary Tharaldson, the richest man in Fargo, notes, "I have created the greatest ESOP [employee stock ownership plan] the US has ever seen." That's confidence. It's confidence with caring, however, because creating his company's ESOP was his way of sharing the wealth with those who have helped him create his near-billion-dollar fortune. "I wanted to share the wealth, even with the maids in my hotels." Tharaldson Enterprises operates more than three hundred hotels and motels nationwide. "From my youth," Tharaldson continues, "I always wanted to create something on a big scale. I wasn't sure what that would be, but I knew whatever it was, it was going to be big." He has good ambition addiction. Ambition, then, at its most essential, seems to boil down to the love of hard work in a business you love. Solving the seemingly unsolvable is hard work; creating a fortune is hard work; managing and motivating a staff of people is hard work; and being a great financial engineer is hard work. But to RMITs, hard work is great fun. It's what drives them each morning with a sense of anticipation and excitement.

Every morning in my youth, my father used to wake me by saying, "Get up, boy—you can't make a crop lying in bed!" This exclamation is the good-morning greeting that I awaken my three sons with today. Like my father, I grew up on a red-clay Georgia farm, though I can't honestly say we raised "crops" as he had when he was a boy. His family raised cotton, corn, and sugarcane. By the time I was ready to work, the Jones farm was not the typical Southern cotton plantation. Instead, we raised chicken and a nice herd of beef cattle. Even though my involvement with my family's farm was minimal—at least that's what my brothers claim—I understood from an early age the significance of that statement "You can't make a crop lying in bed." To this day, every time I even think of sleeping in, I'm haunted by my dad's all-too-true philosophy.

Joe Taylor, the former CEO of Southland Log Homes and current secretary of commerce for the state of South Carolina, puts it this way: "It's not an elephant hunt. I always tell young people there is no substitute for hard work and diligence. It takes eight hours a day of hard work to be a success, but it takes most people twelve or thirteen hours a day to do eight hours of good work." It seems so cliché to say that there is no substitute for hard work in becoming successful. How many times have we heard this from our parents, mentors, and loved ones? Ben Franklin's suggestion in *The Way to Wealth*, first published in 1785, was right then and continues to be right today: "Diligence is the mother of good luck."

While the alchemy of hard work, dedication, and perseverance create ambition and the resultant good luck, Scottsdale, Arizona's Bruce Halle, the Discount Tire dynamo, doesn't discount the power of regular old sheer, dumb luck. "Yes, you make your luck, but sometimes luck can make you. I love snow, because when it snows, we sell more tires. We call those lucky winters, so each winter I always hum, let it snow, let it snow, let it snow."

Luck, no doubt, plays a role in becoming the richest man in town, but it is ambition that fires the imagination of these folks. RMITs make their luck by showing up, by hard work, and by a high-octane ambition. Bob Gillam's voice became deeper and more resonant as he made this serious statement: "When things go wrong—and they always do at some point, for all of us—the answer 100 percent of the time is three words: go to work. Activity and sadness are completely incompatible. The minute you start feeling productive is the minute the depression dissipates. It is the moment when possibilities emerge; it's the moment when hope is once again alive. You can always work your way out of failure, loss of self-esteem, or short-term depression when you become productive."

Jon Huntsman, the richest man in Salt Lake City and a risk-taking chemical baron, comments, "I don't give myself credit for having the golden touch as much as I do hard work. I think that is the very definition of an entrepreneur." Every RMIT in America knows both victory and defeat, but their ambition, their persistence and diligence, and their ceaseless appreciation for hard work have made them the great successes they have become. Says Frank Hickingbotham of Little Rock: "The greatest gift in our life is the ability to work." David Jones of Louisville, Kentucky, sums it up perfectly: "There is no mystical magic to success and great wealth creation, just hard work, dedication, and a big dose of diligence." Benjamin Franklin would be proud.

- Replace bad addictions with good addictions—and in particular, high-octane ambitions.
- Hard work becomes great fun when you're pursuing your perfect pitch.
- Persistence, diligence, and self-belief are the cornerstones of ambition addiction.
- Great wealth is the by-product of ambition addiction.
- Work is empowering: the only sure cure for failure.

RMIT Commandment #5

WAKE UP EARLY—BE EARLY

The sun has not caught me in bed in fifty years.

—Thomas Jefferson

Be Early

The greatest advantage we are all given is youth. It's the ultimate equal-opportunity gift. What do Bill Gates, Steve Jobs, Google co-founder Sergey Brin, and Facebook founder Mark Zuckerberg all have in common? They all started what became billion-dollar companies before their twenty-fifth birthdays.

Risk only increases with age, so RMITs concur: You've got less to risk when you start young, plus you have much more time—not to mention more of what Bruton Smith calls essential energy—to get it done. Ron Rice, who began selling his Hawaiian Tropic suntan lotion on the beaches of Daytona as a young high school teacher, feels strongly about this: "Youth is your greatest asset. It's the last time it will be risk-free." Hartley Peavey began building his Meridian, Mississippi–based guitar and music amplifying business when he was a junior in college. Michael Dell, the richest man in Austin, Texas, started his computer company out of his dorm room at the University of Texas.

But Dell Computer wasn't Michael's first business. He didn't start out as a tech titan, but rather as a philatelist. At the age of twelve, he started Dell Stamps. In his book *Direct from Dell*, he writes, "I got a bunch of people in the neighborhood to consign their stamps to me. Then I advertised Dell Stamps in *Linn's Stamp Journal*, the trade journal of the day. And then I typed with one finger, a twelve-page catalog and mailed it out. Much to my surprise, I made $2,000." Dell writes, "I learned an early powerful lesson about the rewards of eliminating the middleman. I also learned that if you have a good idea, it pays to do something about it." When he was sixteen, he got a summer job hawking subscriptions for the *Houston Post*. The newspaper gave Dell a list of phone numbers and instructed him to begin dialing for dollars.

In the style of a true RMIT, he found a better way. He learned from his random calls that the people most likely to buy subscriptions were those who had just gotten married or received a new mortgage—what is called in marketing parlance "key transition periods." He procured public-records lists from the state of Texas and proceeded to make $18,000 in one summer by targeting the right market. Dell was already a serial entrepreneur by the time he started building computers out of his dorm room.

Pat McGovern started even earlier by delivering newspapers when he was only eight years old. He remembers the book that first fired his imagination. *Giant Brains; or, Machines That Think* by Edmund Callis Berkeley, first published in 1949, helped determine the destiny of this young man from Philadelphia. Berkeley's book "was all about how these new computer systems were going to amplify the human brain by amplifying your memory and by giving you access to more facts than your own brain can readily recall," McGovern explains. "I was fascinated that these machines could quickly analyze patterns in information and give instant insights into the significance of the facts and data, thereby multiplying your analytical intelligence."

McGovern, though, was not your typical science nerd. In fact, there is nothing average about McGovern or his intelligence. He says, "When I got this book at the Philadelphia library, I thought, Wow this is great, because the unique characteristic of *Homo sapiens* is our brain, and this machine is an amplifier of our brains. I took my newspaper delivery money and went down to the hardware store and bought plywood boards, electronic relays, switches, and lightbulbs, and hand-wired a device that was an automatic computer that played tic-tac-toe in a way that was unbeatable. I entered the science fair and won the prize."

It would be the first of many prizes for McGovern. "At the science fair, I was discovered by an alumnus of MIT who said, 'I think you should study the brain as a model for designing electronic systems, and I think we can get you a scholarship to MIT.'" That prized scholarship became a reality, and so did McGovern's dreams of marrying the brain and the computer. While still in college, he saw an ad for an associate editor position posted by the only computer magazine in existence at the time. As you might suspect, he got the prize job. A major perk was his high-level access to the key people in the computer industry.

One fateful day, he met with the head of Univac, the company that created the original computer that forecasted Eisenhower's presidential victory. The gentleman said to McGovern, "Our industry is being held back because we don't have a good database of where the computers are installed and how they are configured or what the future buying needs of the users are going to be." Just like the lightbulb on the science-fair-winning tic-tac-toe computer of his youth, the lightbulb of a new idea went on in McGovern's brain. He informed the Univac executive that he was aware of about ten thousand computer sites at the time; he could call the companies, banks, and hospitals that used computers and put together such a database. The executive asked him, "How much would that cost?" McGovern quickly said, "I could probably do that for about $40,000." The executive responded, "Pat, that won't work." McGovern assumed he simply wanted a discount and said, "Well, if I hire high school students where I live to crunch the data, maybe I can do it for $36,000." To McGovern's surprise, the Univac honcho said, "You don't understand, Pat. No one would trust information as cheap as you're proposing to provide it. Make it $80,000 and we will take it seriously. Information is intangible, and the higher the cost, the higher the perceived value." By starting early, McGovern learned a valuable lesson that he never would have gotten as a middle-aged man. People like to help the young. He also learned to never underprice his product. His company today has revenues in excess of $3 billion—and his personal net worth is double that. Pat McGovern is proof positive that it pays to start early.

Leroy Landhuis, a former air force pilot and current real estate regent of his adopted hometown of Colorado Springs, grew up in the small town of Leota, Minnesota, the son of a farmer who believed, perhaps too fervently, in the biblical passage, "Spare the rod, spoil the child." Landhuis built up his work ethic and his muscles on the family farm, doing every chore his strict father demanded, including what he calls "picking rock" to clear the farmland for planting. A good athlete who played football and ran track, he found what he terms a "noble way" to leave home: enlisting in the air force, where he earned a whopping $200 a month. "It was more money than I had ever seen," he says.

Landhuis learned to fly and actually enjoyed the disciplined environment of the air force (a piece of cake compared with working for his father). Unfortunately, he developed bleeding ulcers and was forced to leave the service, but he never returned to the family farm. He decided to stay in Colorado Springs and build a new life. Landhuis, however, never let those emotional scars of his childhood affect his desire to become a major American success. By his early twenties, he had become a hugely successful residential real estate salesperson. In his spare time, he started buying homes and renovating them. "I slept on the floor for three years eating nothing but rice in order to be able to afford the improvements," he says. Today the Landhuis Company is the premier real estate development and management firm in Colorado Springs, owning thousands of acres of land for development, and his Paradigm Realty Advisors in Tulsa, Oklahoma, manages several thousand square feet of office and commercial space. Landhuis started early, and—even more important—he started building assets early.

A common trait of all RMITs is their early work experience. Air force brat and biotech billionaire Randal "RJ" Kirk of Belspring, Virginia, began selling greeting cards door to door when he was nine. He boasts, "I had an 85 percent success rate!" The richest, boldest, and, at least at Halloween, the scariest (I'll explain shortly) man in Cleveland, Tennessee, Allan Jones (no relation) had a paper route when he was in the sixth grade. He got up at 4:00 a.m. to deliver the *Chattanooga Times* to the eighty-one homes on his route. He would finish two hours later, then grab his fishing rod and fish until it was time to devour a quick breakfast before going to school at 7:45. "I failed the sixth grade . . . twice," he says, "but I never missed a day of work."

Jones started early, and he developed a work ethic that has served him well. During the holidays each year, he led a group of his friends to collect post-celebration Christmas trees, just to see how many he could gather. Ultimately he staged a big bonfire party to end the holiday season before returning to school. By the fourth year of his venture, he had filled his parents' yard with more than twenty-seven hundred discarded Christmas trees. It was the beginning of his lifelong fascination with trees. He says, "I kept a homemade sales thermometer in the front yard posting the number of trees collected for all of Cleveland to see." In our interview, I commented to Jones that he must have loved the money this early venture brought in, assuming he and his buddies were paid to take away the ornament-free trees. He replied, "I didn't make any money on this. I was never motivated by the money, I was simply motivated to be the best of the best." (See RMIT Commandment #1.)

Money became more of a motivator when, as a teenager, Jones founded his first official business with the rarefied name City Bushogging. He took his tractor door to door, offering to mow the large expanses of grass inside the city limits of Cleveland, Tennessee, for $8 per hour with a $10 minimum.

Harvard psychiatrist George Valliant spent the majority of his career studying the predictors of future success, and he proved that childhood work ethic was one of the most accurate ways to predict adult success, mental health, and even the capacity to love. Valliant's conclusion was based on a longitudinal study of 456 young men from inner-city Boston whom he began studying when they were fourteen. As a teenager, each young man was assigned a rating for his ability to work. They were then re-interviewed at ages twenty-five, thirty-one, and forty-seven. The results were impressive: Those who had the highest work ethic rating at fourteen earned five times more than their cohorts who ranked lower. Not only did they far outpace their less motivated compatriots financially, but they were happier and had far more successful marriages and social relationships.

William D. Sanders, one of the most respected real estate investors in America and the richest man in El Paso, Texas, was on the board of the University of Chicago when he learned that the school boasted more Nobel Prize winners than any other college in the country: fifty-eight, to be exact, twenty-three more than Harvard. He says, "What is interesting is not just the sheer number of Nobel laureates that have come out of the University of Chicago; it is their analysis that 90 percent of them did their prizewinning work between the ages of twenty-one and twenty-nine." Fittingly, Sanders wrote his first business plan when he was just eight years old. He remembers, "I always knew I wanted to be a businessman. Some kids wanted to be firemen, some wanted to be lawyers; I wanted to be in business, my own business." He found his perfect pitch and started his own business early. (See RMIT Commandments #2 and #3.) That's why he is the richest man in town.

Whether it was delivering newspapers, working on the farm, or mowing lawns, RMITs didn't just fantasize about becoming successful when they grew up; they got out there and began the march toward that future. Many did so because they had to, in order to help support their family or to have any disposable income of their own, but most worked early because they wanted to accomplish something, to prove to themselves that they could be a success. Buzz Oates, the California real estate baron, says, "I grew up in Sacramento one block from the old fairgrounds, and during fair time each year, I would sell newspapers and collect Coke bottles to resell. I would also happily mow lawns for 50 cents."

Oates couldn't have dreamed then that only a few years later, he would own the very fairgrounds where he'd picked up cola bottles. The fairgrounds of his youth became a small part of his vast real estate holdings. Ron Rice thinks it's never too early to take the plunge into new waters. "You don't have to know everything about a business to start a business," he says. "If you wait until you know everything—something impossible, by the way—you'll never get a business off the ground." When Albany, New York's Karthik Bala and his brother Guha started their video gaming business in their parents' basement, both were still in high school. "We were young," Karthik says, "and we had nothing to lose by pursuing our passion."

Philadelphia's Josh Kopelman says, "I started my first business [Infonautics] in college, because when you're young you enjoy a vastly different risk–reward ratio." As a sign of what the future would hold, he also notes, "I had business cards for all my entrepreneurial ideas when I was seven years old." Inexperience can actually be an advantage: George Johnson, the Spartanburg, South Carolina, serial entrepreneur, says, "I like to hire young people because they haven't learned what they can't do." Youth may be the single greatest advantage we are all given. Don't waste it. RMITs didn't.

Bruton Smith, the richest man in Charlotte, North Carolina, brought automobile racing to Wall Street. But before he did that, he built the Charlotte Motor Speedway, which he opened in 1960. It all started for Smith when he was seventeen and bought his first race car. He says, "Mozart got a piano. I got a car and my passion became my vocation." David Green, founder and CEO of Hobby Lobby and Oklahoma City's richest and perhaps most low-key citizen, recalls that a woman came to him recently requesting a loan of $100,000 to build a business selling salad dressings to the national grocery chains. Green suggested to her that she should just make a few cases of the salad dressing and sell it to the local IGA first. She almost fell out of her chair laughing at what she thought was such an antiquated notion.

He said to her, "Well, I'm sorry, ma'am, but that is the only way I know how to start a business." He told her about how he and his wife started out making and selling picture frames in their garage, and on their kitchen table, while still in their twenties. That little business, thirty years later, is a $2 billion concern giving Green a $4 billion net worth. Starting early and starting small is one of the surest paths to a large fortune.

RMITs also believe that it is never too late to make that crop, because wisdom truly does come with age and late blooming is, of course, better than never blooming at all. The average richest man in town earned the title when he (or she) was fifty-one. Dan Duncan, now in his seventies and the majority owner of the $7 billion Fortune 500 company Enterprise Partners (the second largest publicly traded midstream energy partnership in North America), became the richest man in Houston, Texas, in his sixth decade. He believes strongly that wisdom is acquired over a life-time of experiences, both good and bad. He cautions that one of his greatest life lessons was to stick to what he knows: "Every time I ventured into businesses that were not my main expertise, I lost money. It took me a lifetime, it seems, to realize that."

The average age of America's RMITs is currently sixty-five, proving that wisdom truly does come with age—no matter how brilliant or dedicated you are, there is no substitute for experience. And real experience requires more than a few laps around the track of life. The sooner you begin building that wealth of experience and wisdom, the sooner the financial remuneration rolls in.

Wake Up Early

The early morning has gold in its mouth.

—Benjamin Franklin

To start early, you must also start your day early and show up early. "Don't procrastinate," posits Mal Mixon of Cleveland, Ohio, "because in only two days, tomorrow will be yesterday."

RMITs don't put off until tomorrow what should be done today, and they are scrupulously punctual. Ninety-eight percent cite the ability to show up, and show up on time, as being integral to their success. Punctuality demonstrates discipline and respect for others. Karthik Bala of Albany, New York, says "Nothing is more destructive to one's personal success than the inability to be on time, because it sends a powerful statement of arrogance, self-absorption, and disrespect to those with whom you are meeting." Dennis Albaugh—famous within his company for saying, "Nothing is beneath me or beyond me"—was a very typical RMIT when he set a phone appointment for our first interview; he called two minutes early. He respects his time and he respects the time of others.

Jim Harrison of Tuscaloosa says, "Procrastination is really just the fear of success. People procrastinate because they are afraid of the success that they know will result if they move forward. Success is difficult. It carries with it huge responsibility, so it is far simpler to put off responsibility than it is to accept it." Many of us choose inaction over action. As San Antonio's Red McCombs says, "Action can at times cause pain, often sharp pain, but would you rather have a few sharp pains or a lifetime of chronic, consistent pain? Who wants to be a coward?" Not McCombs. Bob Stiller of Burlington, Vermont, says, "Nike got it right when they launched the advertising slogan 'Just Do It.'" So just do it and do it early—do it now.

Where Are the Best Wealth-Creation Opportunities to Start Early?

RMITs believe that there are more opportunities for new businesses with lower barriers to entry now than at any time in history. George Johnson of Spartanburg, South Carolina, says, "It helps, however, to fall in love with the right business. To be successful, you've got to pick the right business. If you pick a terrible business, no amount of hard work will save you. If you pick a great business, you can be a mediocre performer and still succeed." Johnson's partner, Wayne Huizenga, adds that the new opportunities most likely will not be in the glamour fields.

They're both right. Spend a month in Hollywood and you'll see the law of supply and demand in all its splendor. It seems everyone there thinks they are destined to be the next Steven Spielberg. Every year more than three thousand filmmakers submit their independent films to the Sundance Film Festival. Approximately 120 of those films, less than 5 percent, are chosen to debut at the festival, and only a small handful of those are picked up for distribution by the Hollywood studios. Considering the investment required to make a movie, that's not a surefire way to make money.

So if not Hollywood, then where are the big opportunities? Observes Omaha's Joe Ricketts, "We have just scratched the surface of the effect the Internet will have on business and society." Ricketts also sees opportunities in alternative energy sources, given the world's reliance on oil. RJ Kirk cites biotech, especially human genomics, as a particularly fertile area for future wealth creation. Pat McGovern, the founder of computer publishing giant IDG, says there will be major opportunities in the WiMAX space and also in alternative energy sources. With the proliferation of handheld wireless devices that have the potential to do more and more for the end user and with the seemingly endless rising cost of oil, there are new business opportunities right in your backyard, if you have the aptitude and the right attitude.

How Important Is Education?

Every year, major publications run cover stories analyzing the financial benefit of higher education, especially the wisdom of getting an MBA. Usually the conclusion is that, on a strictly financial basis, higher education doesn't provide a proven return on investment. The personal psychological return, however, may be worth it. Do you need an Ivy League degree to become the richest man in town? Absolutely not. In fact, David Rubenstein—who went to prestigious schools Duke University and the University of Chicago on scholarship—doesn't believe that an Ivy League education or a degree from a top school will make you the most successful person in town. He says, "The only reason people go to Harvard is for the bragging rights." Rubenstein believes in persistence more than fancy educations. Only ten of the one hundred RMITs attended Ivy League schools. Most made their fortunes after four years at the state universities near their hometown. Three were college dropouts (Bill Gates is the most famous one), fourteen didn't attend college at all, and one went to community college. Among America's RMITs, level of education doesn't seem to be predictive of ultimate success or wealth creation. Dennis Albaugh says, "I don't put much stock in higher education. I would rather have someone who is going to get the job done than someone who tries to impress me with their résumé. The longer the résumé, the less I look at them."

But while you don't have to attend Harvard or Princeton to enjoy the American Dream and to become the richest man in town, every RMIT recognizes the value of a good education and makes certain that his or her progeny pursues it. Clayton Mathile, who grew up in modest circumstances on a farm in Ohio, said his mother always told him, "Education is the great equalizer. That's how poor kids get to be rich kids."

Education, no doubt, affects self-esteem, so it can't be a bad thing. Jim Oelschlager wryly advises, "Finish your degree so you can start your education." He likes to "hire smart, energetic people and teach them what I want them to know about the investment business. College degrees aren't as important as a willingness to learn and work hard." Oelschlager places great importance on real-world experience and what he calls "collateral learning," which he defines as "learning that occurs when you go someplace to learn one thing and end up learning something else—something you may have never known existed." He also thinks travel is one of the best ways to experience this collateral learning: "You cannot anticipate collateral learning, but you can put yourself in places where it might occur."

- Start young.
- Show up early.
- Don't let education insecurity hold you back.
- Put yourself in situations where you experience collateral learning.

RMIT COMMANDMENT #6

DON'T SET GOALS—EXECUTE OR GET EXECUTED

Vision without execution is hallucination.

—Thomas Edison

There is a lot of conventional wisdom about the power of goal setting. A multitude of self-help books have been written on the subject of goals and their importance. There are just as many about the power of great ideas. How many books have you seen boasting a lightbulb on the cover? Hundreds, it seems. Goals are important and ideas are essential to success, but RMITs know that wealth creation requires a far more essential ingredient: *execution.* Jeffrey Pfeffer, a professor at the graduate school of business at Stanford University, says, "Doing the right thing is important, which is where strategy comes in. But doing that thing well—execution—is what sets companies apart. After all, every football play is designed to go for a huge gain. The reason it doesn't is because of execution. People drop balls, miss blocks, go to the wrong place, and so forth. So, success depends on execution—on the ability to get things done."

RMITs love to execute. They get things done. Surprisingly, they are not caught up in goals; instead they are masters of action. John McAfee says, "I have never developed a business plan. I have never created a sales forecast, a competitive analysis, a marketing analysis, or a product development schedule. It's not that I don't know how to do these things; it's just that they seem to me to be superfluous to the process of building a product and making money from it."

Often the surest path to great wealth and success is the contrarian path. McAfee is nothing if not a contrarian, but so are most RMITs. Says McAfee, "The success of my anti-virus venture rested solely on my abandoning the norms of the accepted business practices of the time. If any of you have studied the history of software development, you will have discovered that in the mid-1980s every software company was obsessed with how to prevent users from copying their software and using it without paying for it. That seemed like an absurd occupation to me. So I came up with a new idea and decided to distribute my software for free. And even added a headline in the opening page that read: 'Please, steal this software.'"

McAfee's freeware became the world standard almost overnight, and the business was built by charging for upgrades to an existing user base of thirty million people. McAfee executed by creating value, and the resulting wealth flowed from that value (RMIT Commandment #1). He did not seek money; rather, he sought to make a difference, and his contribution provided the by-product: great wealth. Jim Oelschlager of Akron's Oak Associates also built his thriving company without the benefit of a business plan. He says, "I never wrote a business plan—my business plan was to answer the phone if it rang." Thankfully, it did. In fact, his old employer, Firestone, became his first institutional client. He also quickly built a series of successful mutual funds, founded an airline charter business, and started an IT company. In retrospect, he says, "If we had focused on where we wanted to go rather than where the clients wanted to go, we would have failed miserably."

Houston's Dan Duncan strongly counsels against setting goals. Instead, he says, "Just get up every day and do the best you can that day"—a piece of wise advice that he credits to his blind grandmother, who was his inspiration. Duncan believes that if you follow his grandmother's method, success takes care of itself: "Daily incremental improvement is the surest path to great success and a great fortune. You've got to be able to execute every day." His path to his stunning success, and the resulting $8 billion fortune, started in the small town of Center, Texas, and has led him to running one of the largest oil and gas pipeline companies in the world, Enterprise Products Partners. And that's just his day job: He also operates Duncan Energy Partners, manages his five-thousand-acre Double D Ranch, and is a major Houston philanthropist. He runs all his companies as his grandmother told him, by simply doing better than the day before.

Birmingham, Alabama's construction czar Miller Gorrie sees the world through a similar lens: "Success doesn't come from what you plan or envision, it comes from what you do every day. And what you do every day accumulates. That's how you become a big success; that's how you make big money." Charlie Cawley, Wilmington, Delaware's RMIT and the co-founder of MBNA, the credit card company that was bought by Bank of America, is known for his dictum, "Life by the inch is a cinch . . . life by the yard is hard." Philadelphia's Josh Kopelman, the venture capitalist from First Round Capital, says, "We see two thousand business plans a year and I tell entrepreneurs that a business plan is obsolete the minute you press PRINT." He believes that ideas are not what set the winners apart from the losers, but rather a leader's ability to adapt to change and execute constantly in an ever-changing environment.

Sacramento's Buzz Oates also believes that success is achieved in incremental steps. "There may be a thousand steps to it, but success and wealth are created one step at a time. When I started out, I wanted a successful key shop—that's all I wanted." He recalls the time his seventh-grade teacher asked all the kids that age-old question, "What do you want to be when you grow up?" His fellow students offered the usual professions: firefighter, police officer, doctor, lawyer. Oates blurted, "I want to make keys." The class erupted in laughter, but no one is laughing now.

Making keys is a fitting metaphor for the extraordinary life that Oates has led. He didn't just make keys—he actually figured out the keys to great wealth creation. He says, "Don't set goals—take action every day, make good things happen." Buzz Oates started making things happen with his long-dreamed-of key shop after returning from flying missions over Japan in World War II. That little key shop quickly grew into a big hardware and building supply business; the building supply business led him to become a builder and real estate developer. From key maker to builder. From builder to billionaire. "It all happened in steps," he says, "but you've got to keep on stepping. You can never stop stepping." Even Oates is a bit in awe of what his step-by-step approach has wrought. "I never dreamed of having the success or wealth that I have achieved," he says. But Buzz Oates knows that even with taking baby steps, you had better execute or you will most certainly be executed.

Guha and Karthik Bala of Albany, New York, the brother act behind the gaming company Vicarious Visions, were passionate about video gaming. They believed they could create software that would thrill the gaming generation because they were gamers themselves. Today Vicarious Visions is responsible for blockbuster games like Tony Hawk, Spider-Man, Guitar Hero, and even SpongeBob SquarePants. Guha Bala says, "The idea is critically important, but the execution is everything." The brothers also fueled one big idea that they brilliantly executed—better software for handheld game systems. They developed exciting software that made the video experience more fun, more fast-paced, and more visually stimulating to gamers; in the process, they executed their vision daily. The result was that they were able to sell their company to $10 billion Activision, putting millions in the personal gaming consoles of the brothers when they were still in their twenties. They're still running the firm they founded in their parents' basement, but now under the umbrella of a much larger company with a big piece of the Activision action. No one can argue with the Balas' talent for innovation, but what RMITs would admire most about them is their ability to execute their innovative ideas. David Jones of Louisville reminds us, "Innovation is impressive, but execution is what should be idolized."

Much like the Bala brothers, David Green of Oklahoma City believes, "Money never starts an idea; it is the idea that starts the money." He believes the old maxim that businesses fail because they are underfinanced is simply not true. "Most business failures are a result of being overfinanced," Green says. "When you have too much money, you are not creative." He feels it's too easy to lose sight of how important it is to execute your idea with creativity and precision when you have too much money. Green says, "When you have nothing, you have to be creative. When you have no money, you have to execute your business with exacting standards." Like Dan Duncan's grandmother, Green believes that every day you must do better than you did the day before.

Many modern success gurus write entire books on goal setting and the crucial importance of having clearly defined and delineated goals. These books are replete with clever aphorisms like "you must state it to inflate it" or "you should share it to snare it." America's RMITs think otherwise. Once you have found your perfect pitch (RMIT Commandment #2), they believe that daily incremental improvement is the surest way to outsize success and substantial wealth creation. And of course it's best if that daily improvement is in your own business (RMIT Commandment #3).

David Rubenstein of Washington, DC, reveals his first piece of career planning advice: "Don't plan your career." No successful people, he elaborates, knew in their twenties what they would actually be doing in their thirties, forties, and fifties. "The obsession with goal setting and worrying about the future will only take your eye off the ball." He favors a process of making daily improvements while always being open to new and profitable opportunities. This is the RMIT version of the respected Japanese process Kaizen, which calls on us to be in a mode of continuous improvement in every aspect of our lives. Lake Charles, Louisiana's Bill Doré, the driving force behind the deep-sea diving and offshore construction company Global Industries, says, "I never had a goal in my life except to do better than the year before." Oklahoma City's David Green, the founder of arts and crafts retailer Hobby Lobby, is a big believer in keeping things simple. Even though he has a billion-dollar business and more than four hundred stores in thirty-seven states, he doesn't believe in bar codes. He says, "We know how much inventory we have because we keep track of it the old-fashioned way: We count." He thinks eyeballing the goods keeps his buyers' eyes on the prize. They know exactly what is selling and what is not. The retail business is a fluid business, so goals and plans must be equally as fluid. "A good plan in action is better than a perfect plan on paper," he notes. "You can analyze until you paralyze."

Tucson's automobile titan Jim Click is a big believer in daily incremental improvement. Today he owns eight dealerships in Arizona. It all started in 1971 at a place called Old Pueblo Ford. The Oklahoma native had learned the auto business in Los Angeles under the tutelage of his rich uncle Holmes Tuttle. At age twenty-seven, Click bought Old Pueblo, immediately changed the name to Jim Click Ford, and began an innovative new advertising campaign that doubled the dealership's sales in his first year of ownership. Click was riding high as one of the youngest automotive dealers in the country. But he says, "We didn't have a planned-out strategy to be an $800 million company. We simply concentrated on selling cars, selling more than the week before." Then, he says, "We expanded by buying other auto franchises as they went broke." No plan, maybe, but Click recognized opportunity when he saw it, seized those opportunities, and executed daily while his competitors got executed.

Like Dan Duncan, Bill Doré, and Buzz Oates, Click simply put one foot in front of the other every day. Today, the same spot that housed Old Pueblo Ford is his new Jim Click Ford Lincoln Mercury dealership, except it looks quite different. There are eight gleaming acres of automobiles, including a shiny new hundred-thousand-square-foot showroom and the headquarters for his $800 million enterprise. While he may not have had clearly delineated goals, he has executed with excellence every day, and that's why he's the richest man in Tucson.

Goals are good, but goals are not thoughts or desires that march in a straight line. Goals are not linear. Dallas's Ross Perot, the man who sold his copy of the 1297 Magna Carta to Washington, DC's David Rubenstein for $21.3 million, was right when he said, "Life is not an organization chart. Life is more like a spider's web. Things happen in strange ways." Success is much the same. It happens in strange and often unpredictable ways. We must always stay attuned to new ideas, new approaches, and new opportunities. In the end, wealth creation is all about execution—how we make things happen that create commercial success. Rigorous execution is what allows RMITs to adapt quickly to changes. Miami's Jorge Pérez advises, "There is a big difference in good and excellent, and the difference is in the details. At The Related Group, we are great at executing the details. We are famous for our execution of perfectionism. We will not accept mediocrity. Nothing less is satisfactory."

Joe Ricketts of Omaha remembers how he executed a major

change in his business at TD Ameritrade, which led him down a technology path and ultimately allowed the Internet to, as he says, "make me a billionaire." Ricketts recalls, "In the 1980s, we had hit a brick wall with regard to growth in our company and profits. We were growing our business on the top line, but the profits were not improving because my costs for supporting those new revenues were equal to what those new revenues were." Ricketts had a dilemma. He had two choices: raise his brokerage commissions or lower his costs. Since he was in the discount brokerage business, raising commissions would have been highly detrimental to the business. In the mid-1980s, he made the courageous decision to implement an automated touch-tone telephone system allowing customers to buy or sell stocks without the assistance of a broker. This was revolutionary at the time. The conventional wisdom was that most people would not be comfortable with technology managing their investments—that investing required the human touch. Even so, Ricketts was hoping that more and more of his customers would use this service, generating more revenue without adding overhead in the form of additional personnel. He surveyed his customers, and, as expected, they said they would never use such a system in lieu of talking to a human being. Undaunted, he implemented the system anyway. It worked, and it became a huge success. Ricketts executed big-time on an idea that even his customers didn't think they would embrace, but once they tried it, they loved it. In fact, his customers came to enjoy the power and control it gave them to buy and sell securities anytime day or night. This well-executed telephone automation process led him to the idea of using the Internet to allow customers to manage their stock trades. Ameritrade's move to the Internet in the mid-1990s cost him $100 million for technology and $100 million for advertising, but it ultimately made Ricketts a billionaire.

One Silent Goal

Although Dr. Thomas Frist Jr. of Nashville believes the magic of success is in the execution, there is one kind of goal he believes in. He says, "Everyone should have at least one silent goal. This is a goal that is known only by you. It's a reach goal, one that is extremely hard to attain, but potentially life altering, even world changing. These kinds of world-changing goals are realized by only very few people. If you don't reach them, you certainly won't be judged by others—it's your well-kept personal secret." Silent goals do allow you to build architecture in your mind of what could happen if everything were to go right. This sense of never being totally content—knowing that there is more that can be achieved—is typical of the RMIT thought process. Jim Collins, the author of *Good to Great*, calls it a BHAG: Big Hairy Audacious Goal. It's a goal that is so revolutionary, so daring in thought and deed that if you achieve it, you can go down in the annals of history along with Albert Einstein, Thomas Edison, Sir Isaac Newton, or Bill Gates. Why not do it? What have you got to lose? Silent goals can be golden.

- Goals are great, but execution is essential.
- Ideas are important, but implementation and execution are everything.
- Daily incremental improvement is the key to substantial wealth creation.
- Have a life-altering, world-changing silent goal—known only to you.

RMIT COMMANDMENT #7

FAIL TO SUCCEED

I've failed over and over and over again in my life. That's why I succeed.

—Michael Jordan

If you are going through hell, keep going.

—Winston Churchill

I f you are afraid to fail, stop here. Don't waste your time reading the rest of this book. Please give this book to a more ambitious friend of yours. My conversations with dozens of RMITs suggest strongly that *the only way to succeed is to have the courage to fail,* and fail publicly. Perhaps the greatest commonality among RMITs—other than their ambition addiction—is the willingness to face failure and the resilience to pick themselves up and make the next step toward a better outcome.

Jim Oelschlager of Akron, who made his fortune through Oak Associates, a leading money management firm, says, "Don't be afraid of failure. Failure is a part of life. Absolutely every successful individual has had several failures. You learn a lot from your failed experiences, and you will find that generally people are very forgiving of your failures. Perhaps one of the saddest things to see is a person who approaches retirement age and regrets not having taken chances when presented with opportunities because they were afraid to fail." Failure is not fatal, and RMITs simply are not afraid of it.

David Rubenstein, who founded and runs the Carlyle Group, says, "Hope that you fail and hope that you fail early." This seems easy for him to say as he sits atop a multibillion-dollar fortune. Yet he believes it with every ounce of his being. Rubenstein strongly asserts, "Nobody has uninterrupted success. Everybody has failures, and those who have too charmed a life early in the first third of their life more likely than not will not be stars in the next third of their life, or certainly the final third of life. The folks who end up being on the Forbes 400 list or winning Nobel Prizes are people who did not have all the awards and all the success in the early part of their lives."

In other words, if at first you don't succeed, join the not-so-exclusive club alongside such members as Michael Jordan, one of the richest athletes in sports history; J. K. Rowling, one of the richest authors in history; Steve Jobs, one of the richest men Silicon Valley has ever produced; and members emeritus, including Thomas Edison and Abraham Lincoln. It's a very powerful and prestigious club. Michael Jordan was cut from his high school basketball team as a sophomore. J. K. Rowling was famously rejected by more than a dozen publishers before her first Harry Potter chronicle was finally published. Steve Jobs initially couldn't get anyone interested in his first Apple computer; he sure didn't have that problem with his iPod. It took Thomas Edison more than a thousand tries to create his first working lightbulb. Michael Jordan's boss at Nike—Oregon's richest man, Phil Knight—famously said, "The trouble with America isn't that we're making too many mistakes—it's that we're making too few." David Rubenstein, the good political science major he was, agrees. "Just look at some of the recent presidents of the

United States. Franklin Roosevelt ran for vice president in 1920 and was defeated. [He] subsequently came down with polio but went on to become president in 1933 and serve three terms—more than any other president in history. Harry Truman had a haberdashery that went bankrupt. Most folks thought Dwight Eisenhower's military career was over after World War II. He was simply an executive assistant or gofer to Douglas MacArthur. John Kennedy literally had last rites given to him three times, but he overcame his physical ailments and became the youngest president in history. The same is true with virtually every successful business leader I have ever met." All of the members of this failures' club ultimately achieved monumental success. Success and great wealth creation demand that you refuse to be afraid of failure or what your friends and family and neighbors might think.

Fear of failure is the single greatest impediment to reaching your personal American Dream. David Jones, the founder of Humana and Louisville, Kentucky's RMIT, says that the best advice he has given all five of his children is, "If you go to the plate and strike out ten times, you are no worse off than a coward who never went to the plate at all. In fact, you're way better off, because you tried." Anchorage, Alaska's Bob Gillam says, "Success is not so much about winning as it is repairing damage when you lose." Like David Rubenstein, he believes that "there is one great certainty in life—you will lose at some point." It makes great sense, then, to not only learn from your own mistakes and failures but also to learn from the mistakes of others. No one lives long enough to make them all themselves.

Your success is measured by how you handle that failure and how resilient you are. Resilience is the character trait that I most admire in Carrollton, Georgia's RMIT, Bob Stone. He has reinvented his computer processing company, SMI, almost as many times as Madonna has reinvented her look. "We have essentially gone bankrupt three times, though no one knew it," he says.

The first time he reinvented his company was to change from a service bureau that created payroll processing and accounting services for local businesses into a government outsourcing business that processed and distributed food stamps. This repositioning reaped millions in profits, until the government suddenly decided that only banks could distribute food stamp benefits via debit cards. Stone's company was not a bank, so suddenly the very foundation of his business was crumbling. Thanks to his son Joe's insight, at about the same time the food stamp business was looking bleak, SMI was morphed into a provider of systems and tracking for the government branch that distributes child welfare benefits to custodial parents. Today this business yields $40 million a year. Stone's failures were not fatal; on the contrary, they became opportunities for Stone to reinvent his company and revitalize his fortunes. He has proven that whatever forces of change come his way, he can adapt and find success. Stone proves that your success is often determined by the velocity of your resilience. Failure really is your friend.

"Since childhood, most of us have been brainwashed with the maxim, *If at first you don't succeed try, try again*—well, it's true," says Ron Rice, the founder of Hawaiian Tropic and the richest man in Daytona Beach, Florida. It took Rice six tries to get it right. He started out his career as a teacher and a coach, and though he loved both teaching and coaching, Rice laughs about it now: "I taught for eight years at seven schools and was fired six times." Clearly, he needed to work for himself, to be his own boss. No one can doubt his persistence and certainly not his resilience, but it took him eight years and six failures to realize fully what he was destined to do, what he could be most passionate about, what his perfect pitch was. In Rice's case, that passion was for pitching suntan lotions to beautiful women. He says, "My failures taught me my greatest lessons—the most important thing I learned in life was that when I fell down, I could get back up."

The Chinese use the same word for both "opportunity" and "crisis"—out of failure often comes our most stunning successes. Roxanne Quimby points out that one of her heroes, Abraham Lincoln, arguably one of the most effective presidents in the history of the United States, had a veritable laundry list of failures: "He had a general store that went bankrupt, was defeated in his run for the Illinois state legislature, had a nervous breakdown, was defeated for Congress, was defeated for the US Senate, and was defeated in his nomination for vice president, yet he persevered and became the sixteenth president of the United States." Sid Richardson, the famous Texas oil wildcatter who created the multibillion-dollar fortune that is now the Fort Worth Bass family wealth, once said, "I've been broke so often that I thought it was habit-forming." Spartanburg's George Johnson says, "If mistakes made scar tissue, you couldn't see me." You can certainly see him today leading the charge on his newest hotel venture with partner Wayne Huizenga. Their OTO Development Company is building and operating a billion dollars' worth of new hotels all across America.

Meridian, Mississippi's Hartley Peavey, with his characteristic frankness, says, "Hell, I've had multiple failures, and anyone who tells you they haven't is a big fat liar." He particularly remembers creating what he believed was the best drum set ever. To get the high-quality sound that astounded many of the greatest drummers in American music, the design had to be unlike any other drum set. The quality was unprecedented, but so was the look. Some might say the drums were downright weird; Peavey says they were "butt ugly." The famous drummer Kenny Aronoff tried the drums and thought the sound was the best he had ever played, but he told Peavey, "They just don't look right."

Despite the tremendous time, effort, and investment, Peavey couldn't sell the innovative product because the drums didn't look like what drummers thought drums should look like. The design was a disaster both stylistically and economically. What

Peavey thought was a sure thing was a flop. He admits there have been many other innovations that have not caught the interest of the market, but in each case, he has learned a lesson that has benefited his future product introductions. Failure can breed success.

Peavey is an inventor at heart, and that passion for inventing new products is what created a highly successful $300 million company unmatched in the music business. One of his other companies, Media Matrix, provides the sound systems for the Sydney Opera House, the Great Hall of the Republic in China, the Disney theme parks, and the US House of Representatives. As Peavey and every successful scientist will agree, a failed experiment is often the grist for a future success. He says, "Winners learn from the past and let go of it. Losers yearn for the past and get stuck in it."

RMITs agree with Theodore Roosevelt's fervent belief that, "It is not the critic who counts; not the man who points out how the strong man stumbles, or where the doer of deeds could have done them better. The credit belongs to the man who is actually in the arena, whose face is marred by dust and sweat and blood, who strives valiantly; who errs and comes short again and again; because there is not effort without error and shortcomings; but who does actually strive to do the deed; who knows the great enthusiasm, the great devotion, who spends himself in a worthy cause, who at the best knows in the end the triumph of high achievement and who at the worst, if he fails, at least he fails while daring greatly. So that his place shall never be with those cold and timid souls who know neither victory nor defeat."

"Defeat is the prelude to every great success story," says Frank Hickingbotham, the founder of TCBY and the RMIT of Little Rock, Arkansas. "There is no such thing as failure unless you quit, and I never quit. I had several setbacks and I tried to learn a lesson from every one of those defeats, but I never, ever quit." For RMITs, all defeats are temporary; they are rarely down for the count, and they have a near-limitless capacity to pick themselves up, dust themselves off, and set about trying their next big idea. Hickingbotham started as a teacher and school administrator, then worked his way up the insurance sales ladder with National Investors Insurance Company. He founded a restaurant company and two food companies before spotting the potential in frozen yogurt. There were many bumps along the way, he says. "But I never saw a closed door—there was always a crack of light peeping through."

Resilience Is Sweeter

Often the unexpected outside forces are just the incentive you need to make the move to change your life. The *R* in *RMIT* should stand for "resilience." Atlanta's Bernard Marcus, the founder of Home Depot, was fired from Handy Dan, one of the original home improvement retail chains, when he was forty-nine. He and Arthur Blank (also fired) started Home Depot and ultimately put their old employer out of business. For others it could have been sweet revenge, but not for Marcus and Blank. To the contrary. "I always knew that I wanted to own my own business, and it took getting fired for me to do it," Marcus says. "I said to myself, 'This is God's will for this to happen to me and I'm going to take full advantage of it.'" With Home Depot, one of the greatest business successes of all time, under his belt, a couple of billion dollars in his pocket, and a personal foundation that has already given away hundreds of millions of dollars, there is no need for sweet revenge. Signaling both his amazing resilience and his forward-thinking attitude, Marcus says, "I rarely think about where I came from. I think about the here and now. People often look at the Home Depot success and only see the good times, the great result. They don't see all the hard times we had. We had some very treacherous years, and it took a tremendous amount of energy, dedication, and determination to make it work. It's like childbirth; it's difficult labor, but the gift that comes from that hard work causes one to forget the pain of the time."

North Carolina's Bruton Smith learned about failure and bankruptcy early in his career, only two years after starting the Charlotte Motor Speedway. Because he didn't have the capital to save the business, he was forced to place his company under bankruptcy protection. Rather than being the big boss as he so enjoyed, he was soon working for a trustee put in place by the bankruptcy court to restructure the company. Many people in this situation would have been depressed, daunted, and demoralized. Not Smith. He proudly asserts: "I became the trustee's best friend. He called me all the time, because I knew the business; he didn't. I worked for him for a year—for free—because I was determined to reorganize the business and regain control. We ultimately paid off all the creditors and here we are today, a thriving company." Smith is now a billionaire and Charlotte's RMIT.

Notwithstanding two exceptions—Jonathan Nelson of Providence, Rhode Island, and Phil Ruffin of Wichita, Kansas—all the RMITs in this book offered that at some point in their careers, they had failures. Most have "enjoyed" multiple failures. These stories are not isolated examples of a few remarkable RMITs rising above adversity. Business catastrophes are universal: The fact is that 70 percent of all new businesses fail in their first year. RMITs are not immune.

On the contrary, their willingness to take risks makes them more prone to failure than a corporate drone who never takes any chances. But they have embraced their mistakes, learned from them, and persevered in the face of failure. Louisville, Kentucky's David Jones had what he thought was a brilliant idea for making acute medical care easily accessible to the consumer with a fast-food approach. Med Purse was a doc-in-the-box concept that allowed a person in need of immediate care to stop by a no-appointment-necessary facility in a local strip mall.

Consumers loved the concept and the convenience, but Jones and his team had forgotten they had another critical constituency—namely, doctors. The doctors who were affiliated with Humana's hospitals became disgruntled at this new competition and threatened to boycott Humana (Jones's cash cow) if Jones continued to build his Med Purse retail business. Jones learned the hard way, through a devastating failure, that you can't shoot the goose that laid the original golden egg. "That failure," he says, "reinforced the tenet of focus. I had focused on the wrong thing and lost sight of the real gold mine, Humana."

Former basketball star Michael Jordan is not the richest man in his current hometown of Chicago—Sam Zell is—but he could well be one day given his business acumen off the court. Nevertheless, Jordan has said, "I've missed more than 9,000 shots in my career. I've lost almost 300 games. Twenty-six times, I've been trusted to take the game-winning shot and I missed. I've failed over and over, and yet, that is why I succeed." In some cases, these RMITs had near-cataclysmic failures before they achieved their defining success. Bruton Smith's bankruptcy at the Charlotte Speedway could have been the end, but instead it was the beginning of a billion-dollar fortune. The "butt ugly" drums that Hartley Peavey had such a personal and financial investment in could have sent him into a dark depression, or Michael Jordan's failed shots could have thrown him off his game. Didn't happen. RMITs know that failure often leads to their rightful success path. They recognize failure's inevitability and learn from each mistake along the way—and yet they are never totally satisfied with their performance. Just as they don't fear failure, they don't totally trust success. That's a powerful part of the RMIT DNA.

Even when business is good, the specter of failure helps RMITs stay sharp. Although he has built a $4-billion-plus fortune and has homes in Manalapan, Florida, and Grand Rapids, Michigan—all the comforts of a rich, full life and more—Richard DeVos, the ace of Amway, rated his success at 5 on a scale of

1 to 10. Most Americans would kill to have his track record and his fortune, but DeVos points out the dangers of complacency: "Every business and every person must constantly reinvent themselves if they desire to stay at the top of the heap. It pays to be a little paranoid." That's why billionaire Andy Grove, senior adviser to Executive Management and former chairman of the board of Intel Corporation, wrote his book *Only the Paranoid Survive*. According to Grove (who, by the way, is not the richest man in San Francisco with a net worth of $4 billion—Larry Page of Google fame is), "Every leader will eventually reach a nightmare moment—when massive change occurs and a company must, virtually overnight, adapt or fall by the wayside." He calls such a moment a strategic inflection point. "When a strategic inflection point rears its ugly head, the ordinary rules of business go out the window," says Grove.

William D. Sanders agrees wholeheartedly: "Unless you have the most perfect patent in the world, you can never totally relax." When I asked Columbia's Joe Taylor, who is now the commerce secretary for the state of South Carolina, to name the one thing that most affected his success, he stated bluntly, "I'm constantly paranoid." Growing up with a father who was a serial entrepreneur, he said, "One week we were the richest folks in the town and then the next we were the poorest. I vowed then that I never wanted to be on that societal seesaw. For my father, the fun was in the start-up, not in the execution of the business or the day-to-day management. I vowed to be good at both." He certainly has been, and his paranoia has paid off prodigiously.

Companies have strategic inflection points, and so do individuals. RMITs are masters of resilience and reinvention. Roxanne Quimby says, "You can never dust yourself off and say, *I'm done*. Success is a process, and most people simply quit too soon. People love the rags-to-riches stories, the overnight-success syndrome, but I believe that is a cultural myth. Hard work, perseverance, and never being too satisfied or too comfortable is what ultimately leads to real success."

When asked to rate their success on a scale of 1 to 10, 85 percent of the RMITs claimed a number between 6 and 8. Even though the poorest among these RMITs is worth a conservative $100 million, most don't feel they have knocked the ball out of the proverbial park. Harris Rosen of Orlando, Florida, who has recently completed his third major hotel property in Orlando—a fifteen-hundred-room golf resort with more than 350,000 square feet of meeting space, making it the largest in this convention city—says, "If Shingle Creek is a success, then maybe I'll rate myself a 9."

Dan Duncan, who is perhaps the quietest billionaire in America, certainly in Houston—a town where, as the saying goes, money is shown as much as it is grown—confidently articulates, "I'm never satisfied! I always know that I can do a better job, I can live a better life, I can treat people better than I have, and I can and must always work to improve myself." Archie "Red" Emmerson remembers that his father was a hard worker, but he didn't have the ambition young Emmerson possessed. "My dad was satisfied to just make a living. Not me, I have never been totally satisfied." Stay paranoid—it keeps you on your toes, it keeps you pushing for that next rung on the ladder of success. Never fear failure; it is your friend. Remember, no pain, no progress.

No Pain, No Gain

The principle "No pain, no gain" has been made famous by numerous exercise gurus and muscle machines, but it applies even more aptly to becoming truly wealthy. Hartley Peavey of Meridian, Mississippi, says, "I believe that life is a test to see how much BS you can take. The problem with most folks is that when the going gets tough, they stick up their hands and they surrender." In good old Mississippi fashion, he calls it "the watermelon seed syndrome. That's what happens when you put a watermelon seed between your thumb and forefinger and squeeze," he explains. "The seed flies right up—you can't hold on to it." Peavey believes the watermelon seed syndrome is what happens to most people in business and in life. They can't take the pressure, they give up too soon. They don't pass his test of handling the BS that life inevitably throws at all of us.

Peavey sums it up by saying, "Without question, failure is painful. Paranoia, though, helps to keep one sharp. Never feeling as though you have truly made it can be difficult. Yet in moderation, paranoia, pain, and failure are all healthy. Failure isn't fatal. And paranoia can breed progress."

For many RMITs, what Hartley Peavey calls "life's BS" means coming from hardscrabble circumstances or having a family that lost it all when they were young. Leroy Landhuis of Colorado Springs grew up on a farm "dirt poor," as he says. Fellow real estate developer Jorge Pérez of Miami was born to educated, wealthy Cuban parents who lost everything in the Cuban Revolution. "I saw what it was like to go from having everything to having nothing at all." Pérez did not want history to repeat itself, so he pursued his education in Argentina and Colombia vigorously before coming to the United States to attend college at C. W. Post and then earn a master's degree in urban planning from the University of Michigan. Even though his business is the largest Hispanic-owned company in America and has blessed him with a multibillion-dollar net worth, he says, "I have never played the Hispanic card. I have never used it to get ahead. I never wanted to be considered a Hispanic developer—I just wanted to be considered a great developer."

Losers Are Winners

RMITs also prove that being branded a loser early in life may not be so bad after all. Fully 72 percent of the RMITs were less than A students, or weren't the fairhaired children in their families. New York's Carl Icahn remembers that his atheist father said to him while the youngster from Far Rockaway, Queens, was at prestigious Princeton University: "Look, son, you don't have any real talent, you're not an artist like your mother, you're not a musician like me, so you better be a doctor." Being a dutiful son, Icahn went to medical school for two years, but never felt the passion. In fact, he couldn't abide the cadavers, so he left and joined the army. He didn't find his perfect pitch during his six months in the army, either, but he did win $10,000 playing poker. "All humans collect something," he discovered; "I collect money." He has collected at least $16 billion since his humble beginnings in rough-and-tumble New York.

Like Icahn, many RMITs didn't get a lot of parental encouragement at home. Many weren't at the top of their class, either, and a surprising number of them were thrown curveballs of significant learning differences. Even so, RMITs have a way of making lemonade out of lemons. Bill Doré's father had ADHD (attention deficit hyperactivity disorder), though it was not actually understood at the time or recognized as such, until Bill himself was diagnosed with the same disorder many years later. While Bill's father often found it difficult to maintain a job because of his lack of focus, his hard-charging son adapted by channeling his ADHD into action, ultimately building a small, nearly bankrupt diving company into a highly successful, publicly traded global concern.

As a young boy, Doré vowed not to be in the same position as his dad, working like crazy from job to job with little to show for it. While his father couldn't give him much in the way of material possessions, he did imbue Doré with a powerful work ethic. Doré mowed lawns, delivered newspapers, washed automobiles, and even shined shoes to make spending money during his youth. He says, "There was no allowance—I had to make my own way." Several RMITs like Doré cited having a learning disability as a blessing. Charles Schwab, the founder of his namesake discount brokerage, is dyslexic, as are John Chambers of Cisco and Richard Branson of Virgin Atlantic. All are billionaires. Their pain powered great progress in their lives.

Having to overcome a learning disability, parental criticism, failure, or societal cynicism is what RMITs often credit with fueling their success drive. Bill Sanders of El Paso, Texas, today heads his own company, Verde Realty, after having built an estimated fortune of half a billion dollars in the real estate investment trust (REIT) business. Sanders founded LaSalle Partners, one of the most successful REITs in the country, which he later sold to GE. Sanders says of his youth, "I wasn't a top student in high school, and yet I was accepted into the Ivy League's prestigious Cornell University, where I was in the bottom quartile of my class." He was motivated by his early failures to work harder to outpace his peers at Cornell. To this day, he has never lost sight of that try-harder value. He says, "No pain, no progress." That great philosopher and pugilist Muhammad Ali scored a knockout when he said, "Only a man who knows what it is like to be defeated can reach down to the bottom of his soul and come up with the extra ounce of power it takes to win when the match is even." Failure is your friend. Resilience is required.

- Never fear failure. Have the courage to fail.
- Failure is often the greatest teacher.
- No pain, no gain.
- Resilience is the most universal quality among RMITs.

RMIT Commandment #8

LOCATION DOESN'T MATTER

There is no greater success than hometown success.

—Buzz Oates

R MITs are perhaps best described as the rooted rich. They make their fortunes in the places they know best, and their stories prove that success can take place anywhere and everywhere. The hundred examples in this book come from cities with populations as small as 169 (Belspring, Virginia) and as large as 8 million (New York City). In short, most RMITs (81 percent) are doing business in their hometown.

As Buzz Oates, Sacramento's favorite son, says, "There is no greater success than hometown success." Alex Hartzler, the lawyer-turned-tech-entrepreneur-turned-real-estate-developer of Harrisburg, Pennsylvania, agrees, but takes it one step farther: "I happen to think that small towns are a great place to do business and have a real meaningful impact." Hartzler and Josh Gray bought a controlling interest in the performance-based advertising solutions company Webclients, where Hartzler served as general counsel. In just four years, after the Internet bubble had burst, Hartzler and his partners were able to sell the company to ValueClick for $141 million. Today Hartzler is developing the historic areas of midtown Harrisburg through his real estate development company, WCI, which stands for Webclients Inc.—the source of his and his former partner's initial wealth.

Jonathan Nelson loves his hometown. "There is a reason why Providence Equity is headquartered in Providence, Rhode Island, and not New York or London, where we have offices," he says. "It has to do with personal choices about lifestyle and culture. The motivation for starting the firm in Providence was not about money [see RMIT Commandment #1]—it was about having a company with shared values and taking a different approach to the human side of our business. We succeeded here where conventional wisdom would say we should not. In fact, we turned those differences into a competitive advantage. Not starting in New York, having a different perspective, having a brand that is best identified as Providence, differentiates us from our competitors. And it turns out that difference is appreciated by CEOs and investors around the world." Nelson found his perfect pitch in Providence.

Fred Levin—Pensacola, Florida's star trial attorney—made his fortune in his backyard, too. He is also one of the few attorneys who has achieved the position of being an RMIT. Levin is proud of his hometown and says, "I never thought about living or working anywhere else." Jim Oelschlager of Akron, Ohio (population 209,000), notes, "A lot of brokers and analysts from New York City ask me why I don't live in New York, to be in the center of the action. When they come to Akron and see how close my home is to my office, they understand. I am close to work, close to the woods, and I had a nice place to raise the kids. With modern communications systems, you can do the job from anywhere."

Anchorage's RMIT, Bob Gillam, who manages $17 billion of investor funds out of his Alaskan hideaway, agrees: "No one ever told me I couldn't do it here." Gillam's mission at McKinley

Capital is to provide alpha to his investors—beating the bench-marks in each product category, whether it is large cap, small cap, global growth, or US growth. He notes, "We can do that anywhere in the world—why not here in Alaska, where we have three million lakes, which means I have three million runways for my floatplane? Besides, I couldn't find a place to land my floatplane in New York City."

Bob Stone of Carrollton, Georgia (population twenty-two thousand)—my hometown—lands his jet near his hangar at the West Georgia Regional Airport and can't imagine landing it any-where else. The former college professor with a love of comput-ers and a gift for math merged his talents to form his perfect pitch, which helped him create his fortune by virtue of a good deed. The local office of the Family and Children's Services ap-proached Stone when he was still teaching at West Georgia Col-lege in 1973 and asked if he could create a computer program to facilitate the management and distribution of food stamps. He spent an entire weekend working on the challenge, and the program he wrote was so successful in taming an otherwise un-wieldy and largely manual process that the word spread to all the other counties in the state. Stone was in business, and soon his company Systems and Methods was handling the food stamp programs for all 159 counties in the state of Georgia. His only competitor was Citibank, the largest bank in the world. (That's high cotton for small-town Georgia.) Stone proves that success can happen anywhere if you have the right stuff and the ability to adapt to change. But perhaps the right stuff that he has the most of is his resilience. He has reinvented his company three times when the landscape shifted beneath him, but each time he kept his feet on the ground, and he continues to land his jet and keep his fortune in Carrollton, Georgia.

Buzz Oates was born in California's state capital, Sacramento (population 407,000), and built his businesses and his fortune there. Oates says, "I never intended to leave. This is my home." It is, too, although now he owns most of it. *When it comes to building a fortune, size matters, but when it comes to where you build it, population size clearly does not.* The idea that you must go to one of America's biggest cities to be successful is simply not true. From Pensacola to Palo Alto, from Savannah to Sacramento, the individuals in this book prove that great wealth can be created anywhere in America. Frank Hickingbotham built three companies, including TCBY Yogurt, in Little Rock. Former schoolteacher Judi Paul built Renaissance Learning in her Wisconsin Rapids basement, before moving to Boulder, Colorado. In 1968, pregnant women were not allowed to teach school, so instead she began building her company as a stay-at-home mom. Hartley Peavey made his music and his money in Meridian, Mississippi, population forty thousand. Red Emmerson of Anderson, California, created his multibillion-dollar timber and forest products fortune in a town of approximately eleven thousand. George Johnson built his billions in Spartanburg, South Carolina, population thirty-nine thousand and RJ Kirk built his biotech businesses and his billions in Radford, Virginia, population sixteen thousand.

- Hometown success is indeed the sweetest success.
- It's the size of the bottom line that matters, not the size of the town.
- You can build a billion in any town in America.

RMIT Commandment #9

MOOR YOURSELF TO MORALS

It takes twenty years to build a reputation and five minutes to ruin it. If you think about that, you'll do things differently.

—Warren Buffett

Would you rather be the CEO of GE or CEO of Enron? The leaders of both companies were, for a time at the turn of the last century, gods of success, achievement, ambition, and wealth. But Ken Lay was no Jack Welch or Jeff Immelt. Ken Lay, Jeff Skilling, Andy Fastow, and other senior executives of what was at the time the seventh largest corporation in America quite simply lost their moral moorings.

The Enron boys are a perfect example of what Boston's Pete Nicholas warned of in Commandment #4, what he called "ambition without a conscience." Their fate shows that fortunes without a moral foundation are nothing more than mirages destined to disappear faster than they were created. Enron committed the fourth of Gandhi's seven sins: Commerce without Morality. For a time, Enron created colossal wealth, but look at the catastrophic costs: suicide, death, humiliation, or, for the lucky ones, jail time. Jackson, Mississippi's onetime richest man in town,

Bernie Ebbers of WorldCom notoriety, was perhaps the most charismatic cooker of the books in business history until Bernie Madoff made off with $50 billion of other people's hard-won money. Ebbers perpetrated a $180 billion fraud. The result: nine conspiracy and fraud convictions and twenty-five years in jail. He will be in his late eighties when he is scheduled to be released. He became a moral agnostic. This is not how you want to live the last third of your life. Ebbers and Madoff are two examples where failure was not a friend. Moral failure is never friendly.

Moral failures are instructive—lessons can be learned—but their consequences are dear. Tyco's Dennis Kozlowski lost his moral moorings. He gobbled up businesses with gusto and built Tyco from a $40 million company to a $40 billion enterprise, a remarkable achievement . . . or so it seemed at the time. Sadly for him, and for Tyco stockholders, he dipped into the company till to the tune of $170 million for his personal self-aggrandizement, according to charges brought against him in Manhattan's State Supreme Court. Kozlowski will go down in history as the CEO who lived like a pasha—the man who couldn't live without that six-thousand-dollar shower curtain—the man who believed in prosperity at any price. After his trial and conviction, from his jail cell in upstate New York, he told Morley Safer of *60 Minutes*, "I was a guy sitting in a courtroom who made $100 million a year. And I think a juror sitting there just would have to say, 'All that money, he musta done somethin' wrong.'" The judge, the jury, the press, and the stockholders all believe he did. One juror said, "He got his just reward." These are not the results that America's RMITs are seeking, certainly not their kind of just rewards. Ethics are not optional.

David Green, owner of Oklahoma City's Hobby Lobby, built his $2 billion, four-hundred-plus-store, privately held company on a $600 loan based on one ethical principle: the Golden Rule. "My ruling business philosophy has always been, Do unto others as you would have them do unto you." It's a shame Ken Lay,

Bernie Ebbers, Dennis Kozlowski, and Bernie Madoff didn't ad-
here to the Golden Rule. Green, the son of an Assemblies of
God minister, says he started his own company so that he could
create an environment that was morally superior to what he had
experienced at TG&Y, a retail chain that is no longer in business. A good example of those values is that David Green does
not open any of his Hobby Lobby stores on Sunday; they are
open only sixty-six hours a week so that his employees can have
a life outside of work. He cites Wal-Mart's ninety-hour weeks
as a comparison. Even though Green forgoes over $100 million
a year in sales because of this decision, Hobby Lobby is still so
profitable that Green gives away 50 percent of his company's
profits each year to philanthropies that he believes in. The other
50 percent is plowed back into the business for expansion. This
year, Hobby Lobby will open twenty to thirty new stores with
that profit.

George Johnson of Spartanburg doesn't talk about God, but
he does believe in the Golden Rule, and he believes strongly that
"the three most important words in the English language are *tell
the truth*." Salt Lake City's Jon Huntsman says aptly, "There are
no moral shortcuts in the game of business or life. There are basically three kinds of people: the unsuccessful, the temporarily
successful, and those who become and remain successful. The
difference is character." No one ever said it is easy to become an
RMIT, to reach the zenith of success and wealth. Difficulty is
not daunting to these great successes. Huntsman has a plaque
proudly displayed in his office with a quote he loves from former
CBS newscaster Edward R. Murrow: DIFFICULTY IS THE ONE EX-
CUSE THAT HISTORY NEVER ACCEPTS. Having grown up dirt poor,
Huntsman knows difficulty intimately. He worried where his
next meal would come from during his youth, his company was
on the brink of bankruptcy twice, and he has survived cancer
three times. But he never used any of those difficulties to cut
corners.

Karthik Bala, one half of the brother team behind Vicarious Visions in Albany, New York, is sincere when he says, "My and Guha's idea of success is helping our colleagues fulfill their own aspirations." Putting others' needs first often ensures that you become the first-place winner. David Rubenstein agrees: "You should never be afraid of letting other people take credit." An insider in Washington, DC, where success has many founders and failure has none, he quotes Ronald Reagan: "There is no limit to what a man can accomplish if he is willing to let someone else take the credit for it." Red McCombs of San Antonio says, "One of the most important keys to real success—the kind you can feel good about in the quiet of the night—is to know deep in your heart that you have done right by folks." Doing right by folks is one of the surest ways to build what is, arguably, the most precious asset we all have the ability to possess, our reputations.

Reputation Rules

When asked how he personally defines success, William D. Sanders of El Paso, Texas, says without hesitation: "Reputation." In his successful real estate career, he has been keen to change the negative image that many in that profession have created. Today, as always, he values his reputation as his most definitive success and greatest asset. Harris Rosen of Orlando says, "In my business of hotel and real estate development, I'm not selling bricks and mortar, I'm selling my reputation." Fully 96 percent of RMITs cite reputation as their most important and bankable asset. Sacramento's Buzz Oates says, "People have got to like you, love you, and respect you. Your reputation is your most valuable asset."

Reputation has many constituencies, many masters—employees, investors, customers, bankers, suppliers, and even competitors. Bill Doré, the main man from Lake Charles, Louisiana, says, "The reputation you earn from managing your relationships, both in business and in your personal life, is the single most important key to success." Doré started pushing a lawn mower for money at age seven and worked alongside his father in the New Orleans shipyards as a tacker during his teenage years. But no matter how you earn your money, he says, "The most important work you will ever do is work to create a spotless reputation." His sterling reputation with his competitors—which at the time included larger, more well-known companies like Brown and Root, McDermott Drilling, and Santa Fe—helped him become the guppy who gobbled the whale, because he got the first call when his competitors were thinking about selling. He built Global Industries into a powerhouse in offshore construction for the oil and gas industries in the Gulf of Mexico and around the world on the basis of his reputation.

Your integrity is not just a competitive asset—it's also a financial one. Charlotte's Bruton Smith points out: "The bankers have the money, and they don't lend you a billion or even a million unless your reputation is spotless." He advises, "Keep your nose clean and your reputation as shiny as a new car." Auto racing's biggest personality is right—keep your reputation tuned up. Doing right by others always means doing better for yourself.

- The Golden Rule delivers gold to the wallet.
- Putting others' needs first ensures that you finish first.
- Reputation is your greatest single asset.
- Integrity is integral to wealth creation.

RMIT COMMANDMENT #10

SAY YES TO SALES

Nothing happens until something is sold.

—Joe Ricketts

Be a salesperson and be proud of it. It has often been posited that nothing of commercial consequence happens until something is sold—an idea, a product, a service. True enough. But many people (almost always unsuccessful ones) hate the idea of sales. They detest being labeled a salesperson; they often see sales as sleazy, the low end of the business and professional food chain. Old images of used-car salesmen or fast-talking door-to-door peddlers are fixed in many people's minds. RMITs eschew these old stereotypes. In fact, they love to sell. Great wealth creation requires great selling skills. Dr. Tom Frist of Nashville, the founder of Hospital Corporation of America, says, "While I may have gone to med school to become a doctor, I graduated a salesperson. Selling the concept of better health care for all has been my mission, my passion, and my wealth-creation mechanism." He has sold it well, too. In 2006, HCA was bought by a private equity consortium of Bain Capital and Henry Kravis's Kohlberg,

Kravis and Roberts for $33 billion. Frist had billions before; he has even more now.

No one would ever use the term *sleazy salesman* when referring to Washington, DC's David Rubenstein, as he sits in his immaculate Manhattan office with a view of Central Park. The fact is, he is very much a proud salesperson. A lawyer by education and a former White House domestic policy adviser, the private equity investor places great importance on the power of persuasion. Borrowing from his Beltway experience, he says, "The president of the United States is arguably the most powerful person in the world, right?" I nod yes on cue. He continues, "While that might be true, the only real power the president has is the power to persuade—the power to convince Congress to see an issue his way or the pulpit from which to persuade the American public to see his point of view. If you cannot persuade people to do things, you simply will not be a success. Because you are not an island unto yourself, everything in life is about persuading people to do what you want them to do."

Joe Ricketts, the Omaha, Nebraska, success story who made TD Ameritrade into the second largest discount brokerage in the country (behind Charles Schwab), says, *"Nothing happens until something is sold. Nothing happens unless someone sells something, and that begins the chain of commerce."* Ricketts is a proud salesman, having begun his career at Dun and Bradstreet as a credit analyst. It was through this entry-level job that he learned how businesses really work. It is also where he learned that there is often a big difference between the actual performance of a business and its appearance. It taught him something even more valuable—that he wanted to own his own business (RMIT Commandment #3). There was one problem, however: He had no money. Given this minor issue of zero capital, he got a job as a commissioned salesperson for the stockbrokerage Dean Witter. "This was the next best thing to owning my own business," he says, "because as a commissioned salesman, I was in total control of my own destiny. It was like owning my own business, except I didn't have to contribute any capital."

He sold well. With the money he earned from his broker-age sales, he was able to realize his dream of starting his own company. Progress is rarely realized, and wealth certainly isn't attained, unless we use our powers of persuasion to make the ball of commerce roll. Ricketts is right: Nothing happens until something is sold.

Pat McGovern agrees that selling is the fuel for the engine of commerce. Since he began his career as a computer magazine editor, he prefers the approach of interviewing particular customers or potential customers and then deciphering their unique needs. He says, "If my job had been to sell someone something they didn't need, I would not have been very good at it." By uncovering the needs of potential clients and then presenting solutions to their problem—ideally with a product or service that he could provide—he created a win–win situation. He declares that the best sales scenario is when the customer gets what he or she needs and the seller gets fair value for his or her service or product. "That's how you build critical long-term relationships," McGovern says.

Joe Taylor of Columbia, South Carolina, the former CEO of Southland Log Homes and current South Carolina secretary of commerce, loves sales because it is the process that translates a business idea into that scoreboard of success. "While I was running Southland," he says, "I woke up each day cherishing the thought of selling another log home—the whole sales process intrigued me because it brought together every aspect of our business and was the ultimate metric of my success and the company's success." Perhaps the key to Wayne Huizenga's scorching achievement record is his ability to sell an idea to the people who help him make his vision a reality. He says, "I have taken six companies public, and three of those are Fortune 1000 companies, but the key to my success has been my ability to sell other people on my dreams."

Huizenga has always had big dreams—but more important, thanks at least in part to his superior salesmanship, he has made those dreams real. Starting with one garbage truck in 1968, he parlayed trash into several billion dollars' worth of treasure. Waste Management became the nation's largest waste disposal company, as Huizenga led the acquisition of more than a hundred trash-collecting companies in less than nine months in 1972. Under his leadership, Blockbuster opened a new video rental store every seventeen hours for seven years. He says, "When we bought Blockbuster, it had a market capitalization of $32 million. We sold it seven years later to Viacom for $8.5 billion, resulting in a 4,001 percent increase in value." Huizenga found the founder in himself early in life; like Chicago's Sam Zell, he also found the professional opportunist and, more important, the superior salesperson within.

Along with his good friend George Johnson, the richest man in Spartanburg, South Carolina, Huizenga bought and built the hotel business Extended Stay America. This dynamic duo later sold Extended Stay to Steve Schwarzman's private equity powerhouse Blackstone Group for a whopping $3 billion. Today, at seventy years young, Huizenga isn't slowing down, either. He owns 51 percent of the Marriott Hotel in Fort Lauderdale, is the only man to have owned all three major sports franchises in Miami (the Dolphins, the Marlins, and the Panthers), and, almost as a reprise, he and George Johnson are together creating another hotel development company called OTO. He knows how to sell his ideas, and when to sell his companies. That's the billionaire's brilliance.

David Jones, the formidable founder of Humana and the lion of Louisville, Kentucky, says having a clear and easily communicated idea is the single most important commandment of true success. "Borrowing from H. L. Mencken, if you can't write your idea on the back of my business card—you don't have an idea!" He further states, "The biggest key to my success has been my ability to communicate and sell my ideas." The big idea that he sold with powerful passion for more than thirty years, the Humana Corporation, made him a billionaire. At the time he stepped down from the company, Humana was a $20 billion company. Fred Levin, the attention-loving trial attorney of Pensacola, stresses the importance of execution (RMIT Commandment #6) in sales: "Sales is much more than making a strong presentation. For me, it means always returning every single call, always being open to possibilities of what might result from that small courtesy."

Vermont's Bob Stiller wasn't receiving much courtesy from the local banks he was courting for expansion capital while trying to build his coffee business. As with most RMIT companies, Green Mountain nearly bit the dust a few times along the way to its eventual sterling success. "No one ever said the entrepreneurial life is an easy life, but it sure is an exciting one," says Stiller. It probably wasn't so exciting when he had exhausted his entire fortune derived from his earlier EZ Wider success in attempting to build Green Mountain into a profitable business. His new company needed growth capital desperately in the early 1990s, and Stiller sold or collateralized virtually every worldly possession he owned (including his art collection, plane, and home) in order to convince lending institutions that he was serious about the future prospects of the company. This is where his salesmanship benefited him greatly. He never thought it wouldn't happen—rather, he just continued to focus on how it would. Ultimately, he convinced a Boston bank to loan him money. Indeed, it offered even more working capital than the company needed, and that inspired the local Vermont banks to change their minds about loaning Green Mountain money.

He then sold all five of the retail shops he'd opened and began to focus exclusively on the wholesale coffee business. "I had no money for advertising so I went out and sold the coffee myself. I did coffee-tasting demonstrations in supermarkets," says Stiller. Proving that even for a man who had made a fortune in his first entrepreneurial business, Stiller clearly understood the concept *no job too big, no job too small,* and he knew there was no substitute for selling. He says, "I was selling for survival." Survive he did. Stiller's selling skills catapulted Green Mountain into the most successful premium coffee company in the country.

Sacramento's Buzz Oates is a supreme salesperson, too. He remembers that early in his career, when he saw people mowing their lawn with an old or worn-out mower, he would stop and offer them $20 for their old mower and invite them back to his store for a personal demonstration of his new models. He almost always closed the sale and would then deliver the new mower and demonstrate it for his new customer. He believed in building customer loyalty because he had plans to sell them appliances, carpet that he imported from Europe, and virtually any other household need imaginable during that period of post–World War II economic expansion. His superior selling skills transformed Buzz Oates from a boy with a dream of being a key maker to a billionaire real estate developer.

Perhaps the most low-key RMIT I met while researching this book was Birmingham, Alabama's super salesman Miller Gorrie. You would never use the term *flamboyant* to describe this great success story; nor would you suspect that he inherited the sales gene from his IBM salesman father. Nevertheless, in his quiet, unassuming way, he has built Brasfield and Gorrie's revenues from $800,000 in its first year of business to more than $2 billion today, making it one of the largest privately held construction companies in the country. He says, "Intellect is not the most important thing in success. Street smarts is." He believes in hiring and sharing the wealth with what he calls "gorillas"—those key folks who make big contributions to the success of the company. These gorillas have street smarts and stellar selling skills.

Summing up his strong beliefs, he says, "The street-smart people make the money; the intellectuals don't." What do all of these great success stories have in common? While they all have high IQs, they have even more evolved EQs (emotional quotients). They have highly developed people skills, often big personalities, and the persuasive natures that make them RMITs.

EQ Is More Important than IQ

Allan Jones of Cleveland, Tennessee, says, "I failed the sixth grade twice and I made a 15 on my ACT, so I'm definitely not the smartest guy in town, but I can run accounting circles around the numbers guys who I went to school with, and I know how to get people motivated to accomplish things. I believe there are multiple levels of intelligence." Jones has both IQ and EQ. At his core, though, he is a people person who loves to have a good time. My bet is that most of the folks in Cleveland would say he is a lot more fun than his accountant friends, too. For twenty-five years, he threw Cleveland the best Halloween bash in the state right in his front yard. He invented a character called Tall Betsy—in essence a ten-foot-tall, ugly witch (Allan Jones in full costume and on stilts)—to greet thousands of kids and their parents on his favorite night of the year. The Cleveland community still marvels over the phenomenon he created. On the twenty-fifth anniversary of the Halloween party, Jones said, "I brought in the stars of *Leave It to Beaver:* Jerry Mathers, Tony Dow, and Ken Osmond (aka Eddie Haskell). We had over twenty-five thousand people attend, and the local news trucks were there filming for the eleven o'clock news. It looked like the O. J. Simpson trial." The Halloween bash continues each year, though Tall Betsy has been permanently retired. "Her spirit lives on," says Jones. So does his.

Having a high EQ means more than just having a big personality, being a great communicator, or knowing how to make people enjoy themselves. It means possessing another trait that many people wrongly do not associate with selling—the power to listen. David Rubenstein tells the story of two brothers who came to the United States to find success and wealth. One was Walter Kissinger, the other, Henry Kissinger. Rubenstein takes up the tale: "While Henry was a young professor at Harvard, Walter Kissinger became a very wealthy businessman in Long Island, New York, and every time Henry came to New York, he would introduce himself as Walter Kissinger's brother. In later years, even though Walter was a bona fide success story as a German immigrant who made it big in corporate America, he did not share the global fame that his brother, Henry, enjoyed as secretary of state in the Nixon administration. Walter was once asked, 'Why do you speak English so perfectly when you and your brother were raised by the same family in the same household in New York and yet Henry has such a thick guttural German accent?' Walter replied, 'The difference is—I'm the Kissinger who listens.'"

Bill Doré got his start in the industry that would ultimately create his fortune through the power of his sales skills. He was attempting to sell mutual funds to Ebb Lemaster, the owner of Global Divers, when Lemaster offered him a job managing a start-up company that would rent idle diving equipment used in oil exploration in the Gulf of Mexico. Lemaster was so impressed by Doré's sales skills that he offered him three times the money he was currently making selling financial products. Doré accepted and soon purchased a 49 percent ownership stake in the start-up. There was one problem: He was a great salesperson and a good operator, but he didn't have control of the company. Even though the young firm he was running was already generating $1.5 million in profits, he offered to trade his 49 percent ownership stake in the profitable company for 100 percent of his boss's money-losing Global Divers company. He made the sale, though those closest to him thought he was crazy to trade a winner for a big loser.

Doré used his powers of persuasion to build the nearly bank-rupt company he now controlled into a true global powerhouse. Today Doré is the $700 million man. His formidable EQ skills extend to his personal life as well as his professional life. He re-counts some tumult, not in the business of Global Industries, but in the business of the family Doré. After decades of marriage, his wife, Kay, asked for a separation because she felt Bill had too often put the company's needs ahead of hers. The separation ultimately led to a divorce, but Doré admits he still carried a torch for his high school sweetheart. Nevertheless, he soon met a very attractive woman named Connie, whom he began dat-ing and ultimately lived with for two years before asking her to marry him. Six months before his second wedding was to occur, Doré told his fiancée that he wanted to go back to his wife if she would have him. "That was a hard conversation," says Doré. He sold Kay on a fresh start, but after three years, the same company-first issues reemerged and Kay told her first love they had to go their separate ways for good. Dejected but not down for the count, he called his ex-fiancée, Connie, and persuaded her to take him back after three years. "That was one tough sale," he says, "perhaps the toughest one of my life." He closed the deal: Connie is the current Mrs. William J. Doré.

Leighton Cubbage of Greenville, South Carolina, believes—like David Rubenstein—in the importance of persistence in sales. He tells everyone who works for him, "Knock long enough and the door opens. And once you're through that door, treat your clients like kings or queens." In all his entrepreneurial en-deavors, Cubbage has believed that in dealing with clients you "kiss them until their lips bleed." So whether it's logistics or log homes, health care or hotels, you'd better love selling yourself and you'd better love evangelizing for your product or service if you want to become the richest man in town.

Research has proven that analytical success has virtually no correlation to life success, to great leadership, or to wealth creation. You've heard the statement, "The A students end up working for the C students," right? Well, that appears to be true. Eighty-six percent of RMITs graduated from college, and virtually all of those value the experience greatly. *Interestingly, though, they usually value the college experience more for the social interaction that took place there, the honing of their people skills (the EQ development), than for the academic experience.*

RMITs have EQ in abundance. Pensacola's Fred Levin, the only trial lawyer in America to have a major law school named for him, says, "I probably made only 1,000 on my SATs, but I knew I had a way with people." Because Levin doesn't come off as a stuffed-shirt attorney, he believes juries are more open to his arguments. Levin won several of the biggest and most high-profile personal injury cases in the state, and authored the Florida Third Party Medicaid Recovery Act, which put millions of dollars in his plaintiffs' pockets and also several million in his own. That money served him so well, he could easily afford the $10 million donation required to have the law school named for him. But it took more than money; he also needed a great sales pitch to convince the board to give its law school the name of a personal injury lawyer.

RMITs agree that EQ is more predictive of success than IQ. Wayne Huizenga says, "When I hire someone, the most important characteristic I look for is a powerful personality—someone who can get along with anybody." Most RMITs agreed that EQ is where true creativity originates—and creativity is critical to wealth creation. Josh Kopelman, one of the youngest RMITs, still in his thirties, agrees. "I value IQ and hope I have a high one, but I'll take a high EQ every day over a high IQ. Intelligence without an emotional connection is unintelligible."

Having a well-developed EQ is a powerful part of being a successful salesman. Selling is, however, much more broadly defined than the old-fashioned used-car-salesman stereotype. We are all selling something every day. It may be as small as an item on eBay or as large as selling ourselves in a job interview or persuading a banker to give us a loan. Doing all those things requires the ability to see the other party's perspective—to make that emotional connection—in order to get them to see yours. To become an RMIT, it is thus critically important to escalate your EQ and hone your selling skills. Finding your inner salesperson can power the wheels of commerce to create your wealth and fulfillment.

- Nothing happens until something is sold.
- Listening is the core component of successful selling.
- You can enhance your EQ—simply put other people first.
- Find your inner salesperson.
- EQ equals SQ (success quotient), which delivers a high WQ (wealth quotient).

RMIT Commandment #11

BORROW FROM THE BEST—
AND THE WORST

I not only use all the brains that I have, but all that I can borrow.

—Woodrow Wilson

RMITs are smart enough to know that they don't have all the answers in business or in life. Perhaps this is why they are such eternal students—and perhaps it's the reason one of their common denominators is their almost universal interest in reading biographies of other successful people. They value those people who keep their antennae high in the air, and they strive to stay attuned to new ideas, new and better approaches to wealth creation.

The founder of IBM was someone Pat McGovern borrowed wisdom and accepted advice from. Early in McGovern's career, Thomas Watson suggested that there was a huge market in education for technology end users. McGovern took that wise advice and subsequently founded *Computerworld* magazine, the cornerstone of what is now International Data Group (IDG), which brings computer information to those end users. He followed on *Computerworld*'s success by building an events and conference business to bring tech education to both the industry and consumers. McGovern borrowed from the best. From Watson, he learned his greatest business lesson—stay close to your customer. Always focusing on the needs of customers, staying in constant contact with them and their needs, allowed McGovern to build a $3 billion company that today has more than $1 billion in readily deployable cash, with virtually no initial investment capital—only the $5,000 from the sale of McGovern's car.

Always borrowing from the best, McGovern recalls asking the head of a major publishing company what he thought the core principle of the business was. The executive said, "Making your readers successful." That was simple yet radical advice, as McGovern notes that many in the publishing industry think the business is all about selling advertising or making beautifully designed pages. He never forgot that trenchant wisdom, and it has served him well. McGovern is also thankful that a top Univac executive admonished him for underpricing his research and advised him to sell his computer research widely to all the technology companies. With that counsel, McGovern sent letters offering his research to ten companies and almost immediately received nine checks for $80,000 each in his mailbox. Those nine checks provided him the base capital to start his business without having to borrow a penny. Pat McGovern instead borrowed ideas from the best—and therefore didn't have to borrow from the bank. That's why he has $6 billion in the bank today.

Like McGovern, El Paso's Bill Sanders borrowed ideas and inspiration from Tom Watson. He says, "I read everything he ever wrote; I studied IBM and the Watson philosophy on the power and importance of human capital, and it deeply affected how I ran and how I run my businesses today." In fact, Sanders told me that while running LaSalle Partners, the giant real estate investment trust company that he founded and later sold to GE for $2 billion, he hired more than a hundred managers from IBM. Even though they had little or no real estate experience, what they did have was a culture and training that, at the time, was the best in the business. He says, "I even started wearing buttondown collar shirts just like Tom Watson, and I still do."

Sanders also borrowed from one of his peers while he was at Cornell University. He wasn't exactly a straight-A student in high school—and as he describes it, he was "lucky to be at Cornell"—but as luck would have it, he was fortunate to have a roommate whom he labels a rare genius. Sanders knew that he could not catch up to his friend in engineering or physics, so it gave him a powerful motivation to achieve an even greater level of success in business. His silent goal (see RMIT Commandment #6) was to show his roommate, and his fellow students, that he could make it big in the business world. "My environment was a propulsion mechanism for me," he says.

Playing in the big leagues forces you to raise your game, and you pick up a lot of pointers. Judi Paul of Boulder, Colorado, found her inspiration growing up in small-town Baxter, Iowa, through reading books. She says, "There wasn't anything else to do." There was no library in her hometown, only a Maytag factory, but there was a bookmobile that she looked forward to visiting when it rolled into town once a week. The tomes it brought to her town transported her to new and exciting places. She says, "Books made my world much larger than Baxter, Iowa."

That love of reading—which she could not easily instill in her own kids years later, in the video age—presaged the creation of her wealth. She created an Accelerated Reader program that became the basis for her educational software company Renaissance Learning, Inc. Her aha moment came when she called home shortly after arriving at the University of Iowa. She told her father that having come from a small town, she didn't know if she was going to be able to make it at the big university. She whined that her contemporaries seemed to have already taken college-level courses and seemed light-years ahead of her. Her father said, "Well, Judi, if you can't cut it, you can always come home and work in the Maytag factory." She says, "My dad didn't know it at the time, but he had just delivered one of the greatest motivational speeches of all time." Judi Paul found that she was able to compete thanks to all those books she borrowed from the bookmobile and from the motivation she received from her dad.

Gary Tharaldson, Fargo's RMIT, proudly says, "I came from nothing." Yet he builds, on average, twenty-five new hotel properties a year without an original idea. "I like to borrow an existing concept and make it better," he explains. "Building hotels is not a new idea or a new business, but I found you could duplicate a successful concept, make it even better, and create one hell of a business. I have borrowed from Bill Marriott's successes, but I have added my own unique touches. For example, I was the first to put the laundry room behind the front desk so the night manager could also do the laundry when there was little else to do."

Jim Harrison of Harco Drugs, Bill Kellogg of Kohl's Department Stores, David Green of Hobby Lobby, and Bernie Marcus of Home Depot all cite Sam Walton as both a friend and someone from whom they learned valuable lessons. Scottsdale, Arizona's Bruce Halle also borrowed wisdom from the Wal-Mart founder, including humility. "Sam Walton was the best retail mind America has ever created, and I studied everything he ever did to see what I could steal. Every time I think we have done well, I remind myself that Sam Walton started Wal-Mart in 1960, the same year I started my tire business," he says.

Halle has probably supplied many tires to fellow Arizonans, including Tucson's richest man in town, Jim Click. Click, who owns thirteen of the most successful automobile dealerships in the country, says he borrowed wisdom and insight from both his father and his dapper rich uncle. He remembers vividly the lesson his folksy Oklahoma father taught him about quitting.

Young Click called home one evening while he was at Oklahoma State University to say that he was going to quit playing football. Jim said, "Dad, these guys are just too good for me. I'm just an all-American average boy, not an All-American football player." His dad retorted, "Bullshit—I didn't raise you to be just an all-American average boy." Then, after a dramatic pause, he said to his dejected son, "Okay, son, you're right—I think I'll just quit, too. Business is tough; I don't want to worry about feeding your brothers and sisters or putting you through college, or providing for your mother. It's just too much work. I'm done, too." Father Click was so convincing that Jim said, "Don't do that Dad. If you don't quit—I won't quit." Fortunately for young Jim, he hung in and even got to play center for Oklahoma State, featuring Walt Garrison in the backfield. Garrison would later join the Dallas Cowboys as their star fullback. "Thanks to Dad's psychology," Click says, "I got to play with a great player like Garrison—never mind that it was because all the other centers quit the team." Click didn't.

The word *quit* was not in the vocabulary of Click's uncle Holmes Tuttle, either. Tuttle was a member of Ronald Reagan's "kitchen cabinet," and he played a large role in helping Reagan become president in 1980. He also played a critical part in helping Click become the richest man in Tucson. Click recalls fondly that his uncle Holmes was the big family success story, who had left Tuttle, Oklahoma, and hitchhiked to California to make his fortune. And he eventually made his fortune, though like most RMITs, he needed a few tries and over twenty years to do so. His success and lavish lifestyle were legend within Click's Oklahoma family.

Holmes Tuttle got his big opportunity just after World War II when Henry Ford asked him to be the first Ford dealer on the West Coast. His success with that dealership gave him a lifestyle that Click would come to covet and today enjoys himself, thanks in part to Tuttle's inspiration and mentorship. He says,

"Uncle Holmes had a big house in Hancock Park, fancy cars, fashionable clothing." The Tuttles traveled first-class to Europe frequently. "In 1966," Jim Click recalls, "Uncle Holmes was taking his family to Europe and he invited the poor relation, me, to come along. Having never been outside of Oklahoma, this was a life-changing experience." Click's grand tour began in Paris, where they stayed at the Bristol Hotel and ate at world-famous Maxim's restaurant. Then it was London, where they stayed in the Dart family's luxurious flat. After the theater and the opera, it was off to the Glen Eagles Hotel in Scotland, where tuxedos were required each evening. "I liked this lifestyle," says Click, remembering what it was like when he was just twenty-two. He realized then, thanks to his uncle's inspiration, what he wanted out of life—and it was more than a small Oklahoma town could provide.

When his uncle offered him an opportunity to come sell cars in Tucson, he didn't hesitate. He is still selling cars today in the dealerships that he owns with his cousin and partner, Bob Tuttle, and he still loves every minute of it. He lives even better than his famous uncle did. When I ask how his life differs from his uncle's, he says, "Well, I have a nice plane." That says it all. As Sacramento's sage, Buzz Oates, told me, "You've got to be at least $150 million rich to have your own jet." Uncle Holmes would be proud. Click borrowed from the best. In his case, the best just happened to be his wealthy uncle.

Christel DeHaan of Indianapolis also borrowed inspiration from her extended family. She says, "I was inspired by the entrepreneurship of my mother's uncles. Their success excited me. Their abilities to run their own companies proved to me that it was possible." Jonathan Nelson of Providence has, for most of his career, been the youngest person in the room in his business dealings; he has consequently been exposed to many older, more seasoned executives from whom he has learned both good and bad life lessons. He says, "Wisdom truly does come with age, but you can also learn a lot that you don't want to employ in your life and your success." Early in his career, before founding the multibillion-dollar Providence Equity Partners, he met a very successful company founder and CEO who at the time was in his eighties. The man told Nelson that whenever he was sick, he would cross the nearby state line and stay in a hotel rather than remain in the comfort of his home. When Nelson asked him why he always left town when he was ill, the man replied, "I can only spend 180 days a year in my home state for tax reasons. I don't want to waste a single working day when I feel good."

That made no logical success sense to Nelson. "I vowed that I would never think like that or live like that," he says. The man was a legendary success in business who clearly had vast amounts of money—more than he could ever spend or even give away effectively in the last decade of his life. And yet he left the comforts of his own home when he was under the weather in order to save a few tax dollars. Just as we often learn our most valuable lessons from our own failures or mistakes, if we are wise and observe carefully, we can also learn vitally important life lessons from the mistakes of others—even those who have been huge successes by virtually every commonly held measure.

One easy way of borrowing from the best is to read about the best. When it comes to reading for pleasure, Dr. Thomas Frist of Nashville, like many RMITs, says, "I only read biographies. I have never read fiction; life's too short to read made-up stuff. I read biographies about the most exciting, accomplished, and successful people in the world and in history. Right now, I'm reading about Alexander Hamilton—a founding father of our country and America's first Treasury secretary." Red Emmerson, the billionaire timber baron of Anderson, California, says, "I have never subscribed to the *Wall Street Journal*, but I love to read biographies of successful people. There is always something to learn from the best and brightest in America—people who have experienced life or business differently than you have.

Right now I'm reading about Alan Greenspan and John Mc-
Cain." Memphis's Fred Smith cites George C. Marshall as a role
model and mentor even though he didn't know him personally.
He adds, "My favorite book is *American Caesar*, the biography
of General Douglas MacArthur, by William Manchester." Smith
credits his service in the US Marine Corps for the development
of his leadership skills, which he has used while building FedEx
into the $24 billion company that it is today.

Roxanne Quimby didn't have a mentor or most influential
person who affected her success, but like Fred Smith she says,
"I have had heroes and heroines from history that I have kept at
the top of my mind my whole life." She admires two figures in
particular because "both were amazing leaders and inspirations.
I remember reading once that if you are going to be a woman
CEO—since there are so few of them today—learn about Queen
Elizabeth I's life, because she was the first real female CEO.
Granted, she was CEO of the English Empire, but she was a
highly successful one. She reigned over England as their first
female king for forty-five years of peace and prosperity. She was
quite a turnaround artist—she had inherited a kingdom from
her father, Henry VIII, that was in tatters. As the daughter of
Ann Boleyn, who had been brutally executed, she rose out of
the ashes in a very feminine way and led her constituency into
prosperity and peace through her enormous courage and intelligence. I love her in a way that one can only love a dead mentor,
but she has always been a major inspiration for me." Quimby has
also been inspired by and borrowed from President Abraham
Lincoln. "He took a country that was divided and put everything
on the line for unification," she says, "and he was the one to say,
'Keep your friends close and your enemies closer.' He put his detractors in his cabinet, and a lot of what he did can be applied to
the business world and to success today. In Maine, I didn't have
access to female business mentors, so I had to dream up my role

models from history, and I think they have served me well." She borrowed from the best.

- No matter its source, a good idea is a good idea.
- Read biographies of the best and brightest (and richest).
- Seek the counsel of wise people wherever you can find them.
- If we're wise and observe carefully, we can learn from the mistakes of even the most successful people.

RMIT Commandment #12

NEVER RETIRE

Find something you truly love to do and retire for the rest of your life.

—James Hartley Click Sr.
(father of Tucson RMIT Jim Click)

B ased on what you have read so far, it should not surprise you that retirement is anathema to RMITs. RMITs believe that retirement is hazardous to their wealth and, even more important, hazardous to their health. Because their definition of success is about enjoying the journey, they simply can't fathom a life of leisure, of daily golf games, or God forbid of sitting on the front porch watching life pass them by. Instead, they envision a future much the same as their past—a life filled with activity, business building, and continuing wealth-creation opportunities. When I asked coffee king Bob Stiller of Green Mountain Roasters about his thoughts on retirement, he shot back, "I don't have any!" Sacramento's Buzz Oates, who is in his eighties, says, "My life would be boring if I were to retire." Ron Rice of Daytona Beach notes, "I think retire is something you do to your car every three years, period." Like all of us, even RMITs have to re-tire their automobiles, but they certainly don't plan to retire themselves. Stiller, Oates, Rice, and their fellow RMITs believe that retirement is not only hazardous to your wealth and health, but hazardous to your fun, too. When you love what you do, you can't imagine suddenly not doing it any longer. Retirement is particularly detrimental to the self-identity of active and ambitious people. For RMITs, their work not only defines them but is their single greatest avocation as well.

"I want my tombstone to read, THIS IS HIS LAST REAL ESTATE DEAL," says Wichita's multibillionaire Phil Ruffin. "There is always another mountain to climb, another deal to do, another party to attend." A high school dropout whose first job was flipping burgers, Ruffin knows something about deals, as well as about never slowing down to rest on your laurels. In his seventies now, Ruffin recently sold thirty-four of the forty-one acres he owns directly on the Las Vegas Strip for $41 million an acre. He also recently married a former Miss Ukraine, calls Donald Trump his best friend (The Donald was The Best Man at his wedding), and travels wherever the next deal takes him aboard his new $70 million Boeing Business Jet. "Retirement? Hell no. You just can't do it. Why would you ever retire when you're living this large and having this much fun?" Boston's Pete Nicholas of Boston Scientific agrees: "Most great successes never believe they have achieved the ultimate end point. They are never really done." In fact, this belief that they are never finished is the jet fuel that keeps their minds sharp and their private planes soaring.

Iowa's pesticide prince, Dennis Albaugh, isn't done, either. He enjoys the good life as a vintage car collector, golf lover (he has his own golf course in his backyard in Iowa), racehorse aficionado, and boater when he's at his home in Florida. He says, "Retirement is not in the cards. I have created a life where I can do pretty much anything I want. Why would I ever retire?"

Tucson's Jim Click can't imagine slowing down or giving up the fun of selling another car: "I love what I'm doing so much that I have been retired all my life," he says. His father—who once poignantly said to his son, "Find something you love and retire for the rest of your life"—would be proud.

Eschewing retirement does not mean that RMITs are stuck in a static, lifelong mold, however. Instead they are masters of continual personal reinvention. They are not just serial entrepreneurs, they are serial change artists. Hollis, New Hampshire's Pat McGovern still runs the company he started with the $5,000 proceeds from the sale of his car, but he has also invested $350 million in the McGovern Institute for Brain Research at MIT. "Our research has conclusively proven that we are all capable of neurogenesis—the ability to grow new neurons. The problem with retirement is that, too often, people don't continue to actively engage their brains and therefore don't continue to grow those new neurons." He adds, "I often run into friends of mine who have sold their companies and now have millions in cash, but aren't finding retirement to be revitalizing. In this information age in which we live, where we are defined by what we do, to find ourselves suddenly with little to occupy our minds is simply not healthy. Learning promotes longevity."

RMITs simply can't imagine giving up what they love most, the wealth-creation mechanism that has made them the richest person in town. They also know that retirement is a relatively recent concept. It made sense in the industrial age, when brawn was often favored over brains; physical prowess over wisdom and experience. Retirement was not a part of the agricultural society; members of the sixty-plus generation were counted on to provide experience even when they could no longer physically plow a field. Likewise today's information era. Knowledge, experience, and wisdom don't dissipate as we approach our sixth, seventh, or eighth decades of life. For generations that have been defined by what they do, in fact, to suddenly

not be engaged intellectually in a valuable endeavor seems an-
tithetical to our very being. For RMITs, retirement isn't just
an antiquated concept, but a false expectation that society has
placed upon older Americans, and often more nightmare than
dream come true.

Certainly there comes a time in even the lives of RMITs when
they can no longer do certain things as well as they could in their
more youthful years. That doesn't stop them from maximizing
the skills they still have in new or different ventures. Bill Kellogg
of Milwaukee is not running the giant department store Kohl's
today, but he is running his own venture capital business, investing in promising new entrepreneurs with powerful new ideas.
He brings both his capital and his wisdom to these burgeoning
enterprises. Kellogg is creating additional wealth while helping
others achieve their goals. Bob Stone of Carrollton, Georgia, has
turned the reins of his company, Systems and Methods, over to
his children to run on a day-to-day basis, but that move allows
him to spend more time building his real estate development
business while still keeping his chairman-of-the-board eye on
the family enterprise. He's as busy as ever—just diversifying his
wealth-creation portfolio. Chicago's Sam Zell made his name
and fortune in real estate, but he is now making his big moves in
the world of legacy media (old media, as many call it today). No
doubt this "professional opportunist" is growing new neurons
as he learns a whole new industry and attempts to turn around
the fortunes of some of America's most legendary newspapers,
owned by his Tribune Company.

The move from intellectual engagement and cultural excitement to the somnambulant lifestyle in the Sunbelt is not
a choice RMITs make. Retirement may have made sense when
folks were worn out after a lifetime of production-line labor, but
today it simply does not pay, physically or fiscally. Don't retire,
reinvent.

- Retirement is hazardous to your health and your wealth.
- The brain needs continual stimulation—the greatest source for that sustenance is work.
- RMITs are in a constant state of reinvention.
- Love what you do and "retire" for the rest of your life doing it.

PART III

THE RICHEST MEN IN TOWN

LIFESTYLE TRAITS
OF AMERICA'S RMITs

By this point in your journey, it is my hope that you have found your perfect pitch or at least given serious thought to discovering your true calling. Maybe you've written your personal declaration of independence and begun to think of the best ways to be your own boss. If you've made it this far, you've definitely gotten hooked on ambition or you had it well honed in the first place. You've most likely given serious thought to how you will execute on your wealth creation, and you've faced the fact that failure is nothing to be feared and that great wealth can be created anywhere in America—indeed, the world.

I hope that you've determined to build your fortune with integrity the way America's RMITs have, that you've started to hone your personal selling skills, and that you've begun to mastermind ways to tap into the minds and motivation of the best and brightest who have proven they have what it takes to be the richest man in town. I also hope that you've come to the same conclusion I have: There is still a lot to be learned from America's RMITs. Much can be gleaned and valuable lessons can be gained from the ways in which they live their very rich and full lives. Take these tips from them.

Lifestyle Tip #1: Be a Social Animal

Nurture your friendships—those are the most important investments you'll ever make.

—William Rehnquist

Social networking has proven essential in getting ahead since the beginning of time. Birmingham, Alabama's low-key, high-net-worth entrepreneur Miller Gorrie sounds the familiar but true refrain: "It's not what you know, it's who you know." He believes that relationships are what business success is all about. It was his relationships, carefully cultivated both on the golf course and off, that helped his company Brasfield and Gorrie grow from $800,000 in revenues in its first year to $2-billion-plus today. Houston's Dan Duncan, chairman of Enterprise Products, which owns significant interests in three partnerships publicly traded on the New York Stock Exchange, says, "Entertaining people has always been an important part of my business, because I want them to call me first when they want to do a deal. It's always good to be friends with your clients; it's always best if you like the people with whom you do business." Randal J. Kirk of Belspring, Virginia, still remembers the commencement address given by former Supreme Court Justice William Rehnquist at his graduation from law school at the University of Virginia thirty years ago. Rehnquist encouraged Kirk and his fellow graduates to nurture their friendships because, he said, "those are the most important investments you will ever make." Indeed, from what we know about emotional quotient, making friends and building a vast social network is a key to success and a critical component in significant wealth creation.

Play Poker

New York's Carl Icahn built early friendships around the poker table when he was working as a cabana boy at the local beach club. He says, "I watched the wealthy, successful garment center guys play poker and I said, *I can do that,* so I went home and read every book I could read on poker. One Saturday evening, they said, 'Okay, kid, you want to lose your money? Come join us and you can lose what you made this week, we'll teach you a lesson.'" In what would become a common theme in his life, he realized he had the upper hand: "I had read the books and I wasn't drinking." Icahn won over $1,000 that night. His tuition at Princeton was $750 a year at that time. He learned that Saturday evening at the beach club that "you have to work hard to get really good at something." He got good at poker, made some friends along the way, and paid for his education to one of the most elite schools in the country. Poker is the game mentioned almost as frequently by RMITs as golf and even more than tennis.

When I asked Fred DeLuca of Subway what lessons about success he had taught his son, he replied, "My son would probably tell you I taught him how to play online poker, but I would hope I also taught him to be self-sufficient." His son is definitely both self-sufficient and a good poker player, and that pleases De-Luca. It's not surprising, really, that poker is so prominent in the lives of RMITs. It is a competitive game that requires intellect, independence, the ability to read people, strategy, good math and memory skills, and a genuine sense of social engagement. All are traits representative of great wealth creators.

Give Yourself the Gift of Golf—and Tennis, Too

Eighty-six percent of RMITs believe golf or tennis not only helped them enjoy their success, but was in fact important to achieving it in the first place because of the social and business access it gave them. Ninety percent of RMITs believe that superior social skills trump superior intelligence every time. (EQ equals SQ.) Furthermore, getting along is an indispensable skill in business. "Being nice, being a good guy or gal is a start, but developing the social skills that place you in the room with the big dogs gives you a definite head start in the race to wealth creation," says Red McCombs of San Antonio, Texas. Ron Rice, the RMIT of Daytona Beach and founder of Hawaiian Tropic, notes, "I love a great party—it has been one of the key foundations of building my business. Being on the social stage builds your social skills and therefore your business capital. Be a people lover, a people watcher, a people pleaser. Having a sincere interest in your fellow human beings quite simply makes you a better leader, a better manager, a better surveyor of the culture." Dan Duncan of Houston agrees. "Having a sincere interest in other people makes you a better human being." Curiosity is what drove me to write this book—and if you're reading it, that's a good sign it will take you places as well.

Lifestyle Tip #2: Whistle a Happy Tune

Between the optimist and the pessimist, the difference is droll.
The optimist sees the doughnut; the pessimist the hole!

—Oscar Wilde

Optimists reign supreme. Ninety-three percent of the RMITs rated optimism a full 10 (on a scale of 1 to 10) in terms of critical importance to success. "Without strong optimism there is no success, but optimism must always be tempered by reality," says Columbia, South Carolina's Joe Taylor. Your view of life dictates the result. Belspring, Virginia's RJ Kirk exhorts, "Choose to be happy! I hear people all the time—we all do—whining about their circumstances, waiting for something to happen to change their lives, waiting for the government to improve their condition. I can tell you now that will never happen, because that is not how happiness is acquired. Happiness is not the by-product of circumstances; happiness is in your range of choices. So choose to be happy."

Richard DeVos, the RMIT in Grand Rapids, Michigan, and the founder of Amway, enthusiastically agrees: "An optimistic attitude is not a luxury; it's a necessity." DeVos found time to write several books during his long and successful career. In his book *Believe!* he cited optimism and persistence as the two most important ingredients of success in life. As the maven of multilevel marketing, he saw literally thousands of success stories—and not once did he see someone succeed without an optimistic view of life and a positive attitude about their abilities. Alex Hartzler—the thirty-something Harrisburg, Pennsylvania, RMIT, real estate developer, technology wizard, and co-founder of Webclients, which he and his partners sold for $141 million in 2005—says, "Minding the subconscious mind is a definite key to success. When the mind focuses positively, it's easier to envision a truly successful future." Leighton Cubbage of Greenville, South Carolina, adds: "Many people think having a positive attitude is not intellectual. I say it is the ultimate intellectual thought process."

Be a Victor—Never a Victim

RMITs by definition are self-made. Most have delivered themselves from garages to greatness, from basements to owning ballparks. In the course of all my interviews, not once did RMITs blame anyone for their own failures or struggles along the path to wealth and success. Not once did they cast aspersions on others regarding the conditions under which they grew up. They simply took responsibility for their lives. This sounds so simple, but how many people have you known in your life who repeat the common refrain, "If only . . ."? If only I hadn't had such a difficult childhood . . . if only my boss would treat me better . . . if only my wife would recognize my talents . . . if only my parents had appreciated me more. The "if only" sensibility is a wealth and success killer, and those words are never uttered by an RMIT. Eleanor Roosevelt once said, "No one can make you feel inferior without your consent." Several RMITs cited Mark Twain's advice, "Keep away from people who try to belittle your ambitions. Small people always do that, but the really great make you feel that you, too, can become great." Consciously decide to be a victor, never a victim.

Down with the Doom-Mongering

Doom-mongering is dooming, and you mustn't allow yourself to be surrounded by it. If people in your life are bringing you down, you must exorcise them from your life or help them get help; you cannot afford to allow negative forces that you can't control, control you. Fred Levin of Pensacola has seen his fair share of downers in his day as one of the most successful trial attorneys in Florida. He posits, "People without a personal purpose often secretly hope that successful people have gotten that way simply by luck, not by wise action. They love nothing more than to tear at the soul of others' success. You simply can't let such negative forces negate the hard work and drive that you have so carefully inculcated." Levin knows all too well that great success often has detractors. This is why RMITs believe in surrounding themselves with can-do people—folks who share their ambition addiction and are positive influences on those around them.

Quite simply, RMITs seek out the company of great people. Robert Jepson says, "I was raised in very modest circumstances. My parents had separated, and we lived with my grandmother in Richmond, Virginia. Every day was a struggle. As a child, at least on the surface, I wasn't aware of our struggle, but on a subliminal basis I knew that being poor was not the way I wanted to live my life. My formative years were a great motivator to reach up for a higher rung on the ladder of success. I sought inspiration and counsel from people who were successes, who were positive role models. This made me want to make the most of my life. Thanks to the generosity of the University of Richmond, and through the generosity of my family and friends, I was able to begin down a path of real success."

Despite his beginnings, Jepson recognized he was fortunate. Instead of accepting his lot, he says, "I was one of those guys that if we were required to take fifteen hours of course work, I took eighteen, because it didn't cost any more money and that's what I was there to do—learn, so that I could better my station in life. When you are hungry and there are very few plates being passed, believe me, you pick up all that you can." Jepson was wise enough to do just that. He was the first in his family to go to college, and today he is a major benefactor to the University of Richmond. The name above the door of the Jepson School of Leadership Studies says it all. Jepson proves that even coming from humble circumstances without a father in the home, you can live the American Dream. He resides in one of the most historic and beautiful cities in the world, Savannah. He jets to his own vineyard, Jepson Wines in Mendocino, California, aboard his Cessna Citation. He has a plantation in South Carolina where he hunts quail, and just for fun he flies his own L-39 Czechoslovakian-made Russian fighter jet, which he had lovingly restored and emblazoned with an American flag. Ever the optimist, the turnaround titan says, "I wake up every day with a sense of possibility. What could be better?"

Lifestyle Tip #3: Hoard Your Health

Take care of your body with steadfast fidelity.

—Goethe

Good health is critical to great wealth creation. *High energy is essential to becoming the richest man or woman in town.* Jim Haslam says, "I have never met a big success who isn't high energy." Says Alex Hartzler of Harrisburg, "Exercise equals energy." Nothing is more critical than energy when it comes to energizing your success, power-charging your chances for becoming the richest man in town. Success takes both mental and physical energy. High-octane ambition requires it. Bob Stiller, the Green Mountain Coffee king, believes strongly that "meditation is to the mind what exercise is to the body." Stiller insists that you can't have total fitness without the balance of both mental and physical stamina.

At fifty-three, Leroy Landhuis may well be the fittest RMIT in the country. Landhuis is a financial fat cat for sure, though *fat* is not a word that would ever be used to describe this former air force pilot who is as fit as a thirty-year-old soldier. He works out one to two hours every day and hikes in the Colorado mountains thirty to forty miles a week. He says, "I try to keep this vessel in shape to do good work for my God." Jonathan Nelson of Providence, Rhode Island, works out at least five days a week, goes heli-skiing, and is currently putting his healthy philosophy to work by building the $45 million Jonathan M. Nelson Fitness Center at his alma mater, Brown University. David McDonald, the main man of Fresno, California, says, "Success, like life, is a marathon, not a sprint. And as anyone who has ever had the courage to train for and run in a marathon surely knows, you can't do it unless you have discipline and energy. Being physically and fiscally fit requires both. No health, no wealth."

Advocate for Adventure

Creating great wealth isn't just about the money for most RMITs, it's about the adventure of the voyage—adventure in businesses and adventure in personal time as well. Bob Gillam of Anchorage, Alaska, says, "The best books I have ever read were about Tom Sawyer and Huck Finn because they taught me about adventure." He likes to floatplane into the wilds of Alaska, where he has fished every major stream. He navigates his way through virtually all three million lakes in the remote regions and uses them as his personal water runways. Gillam remembers riding his bicycle to the local airport as a boy because a rare Boeing 707 was scheduled to land. *Wow*, he thought, *one day I want to fly one of those.* "Today I've got a hangar full of them." An astounding 72 percent of RMITs have their own plane; 35 percent can even fly them.

Jonathan Nelson goes extreme heli-skiing, most recently on the virgin snow of Greenland, where he says brave souls can ski right down to the ocean because it snows at sea level there. Bob Jepson loves to shoot sporting clays when he isn't flying his L-39 fighter plane. He says, "Shooting sporting clays requires real concentration, and it helps develop quick reflexes, patience, and at times a healthy dose of humility. Shooting sporting clays is a lot like running a business. You wait for each opportunity to present itself. Then you lead the target: You anticipate where the clay is going to be, swing through it, and then take your shot. You get one chance to put your shot pattern and the target together. Accuracy and timing are important, and you have to work for every point you score. It's like business. It's like life."

Lifestyle Tip #4: Loathe Leverage

Most failure occurs because of two things: liquor and leverage.

—Warren Buffett

Warren Buffett is worth $60 billion because he knows the downside of leverage and the devastation caused by living outside your means. Like many RMITs, he eschews borrowing money. He says, "If you're smart enough, you're going to make a lot of money without borrowing." RMITs don't spend much time at the tables in Las Vegas—unless they're Sheldon Adelson, Kirk Kerkorian, or Phil Ruffin, who make their billions off those who do. In fact, when asked what's their favorite city in the world, the majority of RMITs cited their hometown. When asked their least favorite city, Las Vegas was the hands-down winner. RMITs believe that you can't gamble to greatness.

There is an exception to every rule, as they say, and Carl Icahn is that exception. He did roll the dice—or, perhaps more accurately, play the right cards. While he was at Princeton University, his father told him he didn't have any real talent. "You're not an artist like your mother, you're not a musician like me, so you better be a doctor," he said. Icahn went to medical school for two years, but never felt the passion, so he joined the army. Although he didn't find his perfect pitch during his six-month stint in the military either, he did win $10,000 playing poker. This tidy sum gave him a nice nest egg to begin his first job on Wall Street in 1961 trading convertible bonds at Dreyfus.

"In those days, I was making fifty, sixty, seventy thousand bucks. I even got up to $100,000 at one point, and I learned a real lesson about leverage," he says. "I went out and bought a white Ford Galaxy convertible, had the beautiful girlfriend, and then in 1962 the crash came, and in one day I lost everything." Today as he sits on his multibillion-dollar fortune, he jokes, "I'm not sure what went first, the car or the girl. Probably the girl." He learned that living large on leverage can change your life, and not in a good way, with one market crash.

RMITs have become the wealth winners in their respective towns because they usually think before they spend and weigh the consequences before they borrow. Dan Duncan of Houston, today worth $8 billion, remembers that his scariest time in business was in the late 1970s and early 1980s when he secured $500 million of bank financing to build his business assets, thinking interest rates could never go higher than 10 to 12 percent. Unfortunately for Duncan, interest rates hit 22 percent. Suddenly the man who thought he worked for himself was working for the banks.

"Once I worked my way out of that bind, I never let it happen again," says Duncan. He also points out that the banks don't want to lend to you when you need money. As counterintuitive as it might sound, Duncan wisely says, "You should only borrow money when you don't need it, because when you do, they won't be very friendly to you."

Red Emmerson of Anderson, California, says, "One of the keys to great success is self-discipline. And that means you can't overspend." Emmerson's advice is so simple and yet so difficult for so many people. American credit card debt is currently at an all-time high: more than $60 billion. The average family owes more than $8,000. While RMITs take credit risk on their businesses for strategic reasons, they make darn certain they never take risks in their personal spending. Hartley Peavey of Meridian, Mississippi, says that his Depression-era dad taught him the value of a dollar. "My father was so tight he could squeeze a nickel and make the buffalo yell," he jokes. "When he sent me off to college, he honestly thought I should and could live on $12 a week. That wasn't even beer money, so I worked several jobs because I wanted more for myself than my dad wanted for me."

Lifestyle Tip #5: Look the Part

One's self-image is very important because if that's in good shape, then you can do anything, or practically anything.

—Sir John Gielgud

Will Rogers once said that you never get a second chance to make a good first impression. Appearance matters. A healthy self-image is a key aspect of making a good impression, and it is a common trait of RMITs. Like Sir John Gielgud, RMITs believe that the way you view yourself has a lot to do with how others view you. Economists tell us that the taller you are, the greater your odds of financial success (the average height of an RMIT is six foot one). There is also a strong correlation between beauty and bucks. The better looking you are (the lucky few), the better your chance of success, and the better groomed you are—again, the better your chance for economic independence. To the extent that they are under your control, these traits show attention to detail and personal pride.

Ron Rice of Daytona Beach, Florida, admits, "Maybe it's because one of Hawaiian Tropic's major promotions is the Miss Hawaiian Tropic beauty contest, and maybe I am more interested in appearance than most, but when everything else is even, if I have the choice of an attractive employee over an unkempt one, I'll always choose the attractive one. Taking care of yourself shows self-respect, and who doesn't want that kind of employee or business associate?" Alex Hartzler of Harrisburg, Pennsylvania, says modestly, "Thank God appearance wasn't a condition for success in my case. But I do believe that the good-looking people in life have an easier, perhaps surer shot at the top rungs of the success ladder. As such, I guess I will always be like Avis and will just have to try harder." Nevertheless, Phil Ruffin of Wichita (and now Las Vegas as well) believes good looks don't matter to a real entrepreneur or wealth creator. He says, "Some of us rich guys are the ugliest things you have ever seen."

Lifestyle Tip #6: Happy Wife, Happy Life

*A happy marriage has in it all the pleasures of friendships,
all the enjoyment of sense and reason—and indeed all the
sweets of life.*

—Joseph Addison

Among RMITs, 86 percent are convinced that a happy marriage is one of the keys to success—both business success and success in life. In fact, 71 percent are still married to their first spouse, and only ten of the hundred RMITs have experienced divorce. Dr. Thomas Frist, the co-founder of HCA in Nashville, believes your spouse should be your partner for life, so choose well. He says, "If my forty-three-year marriage had not worked, it would be the most devastating failure I could imagine." In a powerful display of putting his money where his belief is, he bestowed 50 percent of his stock in HCA on his wife at the startup of the company.

Bill Sanders of El Paso says, "I'm still married to my first wife of thirty-plus happy years who is my true partner in life. I can't imagine having the success I have had without her." Bharat Desai, the Fisher Island, Florida, RMIT, is a billionaire today at least in part because his wife, Neerja Sethi, started Syntel with him when they were in graduate school at the University of Michigan. Desai gives credit where credit is due: "My wife, Neerja, is the smart one of us. She's my business partner, plus she raised the children." Bernie Marcus of Home Depot fame, the richest man in Atlanta, echoes that sentiment. "I have been married to my second wife for over thirty years and Billi is my true partner, but before we got married, I made sure she knew what the life of a retailer was like. She was well aware I would be traveling constantly. She accepted the retailer's wife's life and has been my greatest support." He adds, "Not once did Billi nag me. In fact, she spoke at Home Depot employee meetings about the job of the supportive spouse. The Home Depot employees were so impressed because she and I shared exactly the same values."

Jim Harrison of Tuscaloosa gives his wife total credit, as do so many RMITs, for the bulk of raising the children and providing an environment where he could achieve without feeling guilty for it. He says, "Peggy was and is the emotional and spiritual support that allowed me to do what I do best, which is build things." Omaha's Joe Ricketts notes, "If I had been married to anybody else, I would have been divorced three or four times. My wife gets me. I have devoted my life to the two things that make me happy: my family and my work. Marlene always understood the sacrifice that success required and never once became upset or irritated by it. One time, I had gotten myself in a jam and I had to ask her to go to work, even though we had four kids at home. She never once complained. She just did it." Iowa's chemical king, Dennis Albaugh, recalls that when he applied for his first $10,000 SBA (Small Business Association) loan, his wife had to agree to second-mortgage their house. The local bankers actually came to their home and explained to Susan that the bank would have to take their house if Albaugh's business went bust. She promptly co-signed the note, and many thereafter. He says, "Susan has been my success partner in every way, all along the way."

Jim Oelschlager's wife, Vanita, epitomizes the supportive spouse. Given Jim's physical limitations due to his MS, she is constantly by his side. She works alongside him at his investment company, Oak Associates; when he travels, she serves as his legs. She has even found time to write five books that are at least in part about Jim. *Air Mask*, a book of poems, deals poignantly and honestly about the trials, frustrations, and joys of being constantly in the caretaker role. Despite—or perhaps even because of—all the difficulties each has endured, their partnership remains strong. This is exactly what Oelschlager means when he utters one of his favorite sayings, "Get a good partner and have a good partnership."

Fourteen percent of RMITs, however, say that it's better to put off relationships and family until you have truly made it. Joe Taylor, of Columbia, South Carolina, maintains that "when building a business with a goal of creating sizable wealth, relationships will undoubtedly suffer." Taylor, who didn't marry until he was thirty-five, advises young entrepreneurs to wait until they're successful. Another prominent RMIT who shares that belief is hotel developer Harris Rosen, the richest man in Orlando, Florida, who didn't marry until he was fifty.

Lifestyle Tip #7: Sex: What's Good in the Bedroom Is Great in the Boardroom

Wealth is the ultimate aphrodisiac.

—Anonymous RMIT

One way of looking at the passion so critical to success is to understand that sex drive often predicts and parallels success drive. Getting any of America's RMITs to discuss their sex lives was a delicate proposition and a difficult task. However, off the record and sometimes over a drink at the end of their long day, more than a dozen RMITs offered that they were as passionate in their sex lives as they were in building their businesses and their wealth.

One memorable RMIT said, "My sex drive and my business drive are co-dependent. Wealth is the ultimate aphrodisiac." This highly charged sex drive is not surprising, really, considering the science that corroborates my findings. It could be as simple as testosterone, the male sex hormone often thought of as the "aggression hormone."

In 2008, two University of Cambridge neuroscience researchers, Joe Herbert and John Coates, sampled saliva from seventeen stock traders to determine the relationship between testosterone level and trading success. The result? The men with higher levels of testosterone were more successful—as defined in this study as those who made the most money. Passion is, without question, a universal trait of the most successful self-made men and women in America—no matter whether it's for business, for wealth, or for love. Properly channeled passion in both the bedroom and the boardroom is highly predictive of wealth creation. The desire for financial gain is often as alluring as the lure of sex.

Lifestyle Tip #8: God and Money

God promises a hundredfold return for anything we invest in him.

—Leroy Landhuis

Albert Einstein posited: "There are only two ways to live your life. One is as though nothing is a miracle. The other is as if everything is." Faith seems to be a prerequisite for living a life populated with miracles. The majority of RMITs cite faith as having played a role in their success. Three give all the credit to God. Leroy Landhuis of Colorado Springs, David Green of Oklahoma City, and Buzz Oates of Sacramento all believe their success is the grand plan of their God. Oates remarked humbly and honestly, "The Lord has always been faithful to me. I haven't always been faithful to him." Oates has been faithful to Joel Osteen's ministry both spiritually and financially. He takes his private jet to Lakewood Church in Houston, Texas (the largest nondenominational church in the country, with thirty thousand members), to hear the gospel from the Osteen family, whom he considers friends.

Oates has also recently given $3 million to Mercy Ministries (the international Christian charity founded by Nancy Alcorn that helps young troubled women) to build a center in Sacramento. He says, "I realize the Lord was instrumental in bringing me the profits that I have now, and I want to use those profits for him to change the world."

So does Leroy Landhuis of Colorado Springs. Though fiercely private about his good deeds, he does admit that he has and is building orphanages, schools, churches, and hospitals to do God's work all over the world, especially in Africa. He says, "That's what I do with my money. When I was in my twenties, men took time to meet with and introduce me to the concept that God understood capitalism. If you read Mark and Matthew, God promises a hundredfold return for anything we invest in him. Being a guy like me who is a capitalist, that means 10,000 percent times forever, so why would I do anything else?" He admits that even though he has a deep and abiding belief in God and a determined desire to fulfill God's grand plan for him, "That is not where I have spent all my time, so I am dumber than you might think. If you had known this you probably wouldn't have called me to be a part of your book." He wants to encourage other men to pursue a relationship with the God who created them and loved them: "We're all going to die and you want to make sure you've invested your life wisely." Landhuis isn't as saintly as he sounds. He candidly offers, "I have not been a success in my personal life the way I would have liked to be. My marriage wasn't successful and at times, I have been much too occupied with business. Up until recently, I haven't opened up emotionally." He adds, "In the Midwest where I grew up, you don't have any philosophical or emotional discussions about anything." The Colorado capitalist with a deep love for God has reconciled the God-and-money conundrum that plagues so many. He says, "Growing up in a very structured home with no indoor plumbing, did I want to be a millionaire? Yes I did. But now I am using my money for God's work."

Bob Stiller of Burlington, Vermont, has been faithful to his spirituality, which he says has permeated every aspect of his life. "My spiritual intention brings another level of consciousness and creativity to all that I do." He believes that "what you think about, you bring about." He has thought about building a great company, and he has. He has thought about having the finer amenities of life, and he has; and he has thought about the personal growth of the employees who have helped him achieve his success. He says, "My greatest joy is seeing my employees grow personally and seeing them be able to make a difference in the world. We have proved at Green Mountain that you can value spirituality, save the world, and maximize profits simultaneously."

David Green of Oklahoma City agrees. Even though he sits atop a thriving retail empire and a multibillion-dollar fortune, he remembers a time in the mid-1980s when God taught him a lesson. Green had gotten caught up in the wave of the 1980s abundance. Oil was enjoying record highs, and folks were living large in Oklahoma and Texas. In his book *More than a Hobby*, Green says it was a time when Mercedes and Rolls-Royce dealers were selling every car they could get their hands on and Rolex watches were flying out the doors of jewelry stores. Consequently, Green started to sell more upscale things like expensive signed and numbered artwork. "We were coasting on a false sense of security," he says. What goes up must come down, and suddenly the high-rolling economy was rolling the wrong way for Green's merchandising. His business suffered so much that he suddenly couldn't pay his stores' utility bills. In one memorable incident, Oklahoma Gas and Electric showed up at one of Green's stores demanding a $3,600 payment—or else the lights would be shut off.

The store manager begged for one more day, expecting that he could pay the bill with the sales proceeds from that day if they were able to stay open. Green remembers crawling under his desk so he could pray to God without distraction or notice.

He then called his family together to say that it looked as though the business was going belly-up. Green recalls his son saying to him, "Our faith is not in you, Dad; it's in God." He remembers, "I learned that I had to become small so God could become big."

With massive downsizing, cost-cutting, and the help of their God, Green steered Hobby Lobby back to profitability. Being small so God could be big is a lesson he has never forgotten. "Up until this time," he says, "I had always given God credit for our success, but I'm afraid it was mostly lip service. I saw where I could truly wind up without God's help. I also learned that crisis prayer is okay, but daily prayer is better."

Lifestyle Tip #9: Be an Eternal Student

Twenty years from now you will be more disappointed by the things that you didn't do than by the ones you did do. So throw off the bowlines. Sail away from the safe harbor. Catch the trade winds in your sails. Explore. Dream. Discover.

—Mark Twain

As you have witnessed countless times through this book, RMITs have an insatiable curiosity. They believe like Samuel Johnson that "curiosity is one of the most permanent and certain characteristics of a vigorous intellect." They are the ultimate lifelong learners. They believe, as Henry Ford did, that "anyone who stops learning is old, whether at twenty or eighty. Anyone who keeps learning stays young. The greatest thing in life is to keep your mind young." Continual learning is not compulsory, but then again neither is survival. "The world is changing faster than it ever has," says Randal J. Kirk, the biotech billionaire who calls Belspring, Virginia, home. Kirk believes that to be successful over the course of our lives, we must be prepared to change careers several times, and that requires being eternal students. He says, "We're already at a point where we're seeing entire industries come and go in four to six years, so a young person can reasonably expect six to ten careers." Unless of course, you choose not to be an eternal student. In this era of constant change, you must be ready to adapt.

According to Hollis, New Hampshire, publishing magnate Pat McGovern, who has funded the McGovern Brain Institute for Brain Research at MIT, researchers have proven that by actively learning new things, visiting new places, and having new experiences, you are, in effect, actually growing new brain cells and therefore increasing your mental depth and dexterity. McGovern says, "That process of neurogenesis increases your immune system and creates chemical messages sent to the rest of the body that improve your health and lower your anxiety. Learning promotes longevity." That's a powerful reason to stay in school for life.

Jim Oelschlager calls being an eternal student collateral learning and notes how often you may find yourself learning things you didn't necessarily set out to learn. To that end, travel is an incomparable experience. He says: "Sometimes you need another view of the world, a more exhilarating environment, in order to find your greatest inspiration."

That was certainly the case for Christel DeHaan. The German immigrant and former English nanny always had the desire to understand the larger world. She says, "I went to England to perfect my English and to begin my journey of understanding a globalized world. I have always loved the concept of being a student of the world." It's no surprise, then, that she would later co-found a business (Resort Condominiums International) capitalizing on the concept of globalization long before *globalization* became a business page buzzword. Jon Huntsman made it a family tradition to give all fifty-six (yes, 56) grandchildren a collateral learning trip to San Francisco when each turns ten years old: "It's a rite of passage to ride the cable cars, see the Cannery, Alcatraz, and all that San Francisco offers."

Omaha's greatest eternal student, Joe Ricketts, says, "It took me ten years to graduate from college because I had to work my way through school, but I learned two things well . . . the power of compounded interest, and the power of continual education." He goes on: "I'm still learning every day. I learn through travel, I learn from investing in new, young companies, and I'm learning from starting a new technology business myself. I can't imagine life without learning." The Internet made Ricketts a billionaire. He says, "It also made me smarter, no doubt, because of the easy access to knowledge about anything and everything that is of interest—and I have a lot of interests." Phil Knight, the richest man in Portland, Oregon, and the founder of Nike, believes so strongly in being a student for life that he has gone back to his alma mater, Stanford University, where he's taking writing classes.

Lifestyle Tip #10: Give as Good as You Got

We make a living by what we get; we make a life by what we give.

—Winston Churchill

RMITs have amassed a collective fortune of over $355 billion and given away almost half of it. The Bill and Melinda Gates Foundation directs more than $37.3 billion principally toward what Bill Gates has termed the "Big Three" diseases: malaria, tuberculosis, and HIV/AIDS. Another $40 billion or so is also coming from Warren Buffett, which will more than double the size of what is already the largest foundation in the world. Today Gates is devoting the majority of his time to making a difference through his and Melinda's foundation; thus he's stepped down from the day-to-day management of Microsoft. He has said, "I actually thought that it would be a little confusing during the same period of your life to be in one meeting when you're trying to make money, and then go to another meeting where you're giving it away."

What do most RMITs plan to do with their riches? Philanthropy is a passion for most. Giving back to the world in myriad ways is yet another job they have taken on. It's their way of saying thank you to the world that has given them so much.

Most RMITs believe they are all simply caretakers for their wealth for the period of their lifetime—that their money is never truly owned by them. Their fortune is simply in their custody while they are here on earth. You must possess it, however—albeit temporarily—to give it away. Leroy Landhuis says, "The money, just like Solomon said, will be left to somebody else or to some other thing and I won't matter. We can't take it with us, but we can send it ahead. That's one of the greatest discoveries of study that I've ever had."

He is sending his money ahead, especially to Africa, while he's around to see the fruits of his hard work positively affect others less fortunate. He says, "If you want to give your money away when you're dead, that's fine, but that doesn't mean anything to God because he's got enough money. If you'll give it away while you're living, he gives us credit for that forever. If you don't believe in him, you won't do it, though, because you won't do what you can't see or believe. It's too illogical for your human mind to grasp. You won't give away millions of dollars to change the lives of others unless you have real faith in God." Landhuis does believe. He believes in God and he believes that his money is nothing more than a tool to do God's work. He says proudly, "God is a capitalist."

Bob Jepson of Savannah says that in his early years, he thought that if he were to be remembered for anything, it would be for resuscitating a bunch of tired old companies—and in so doing making a small scratch on the landscape of American business.

Now, he says, "As I have gotten older and perhaps wiser, I think those of us who are remembered, if we are remembered, will be remembered for what we have done for others, not by what success we had in doing for ourselves." A particularly poignant experience occurred early in his career when he was working in Chicago and living in the suburb of Barrington, Illinois. One evening his wife did not pick him up at the train station, as was normally her custom. He was forced to walk the three miles home. He walked right through the town cemetery, and since it was a nice day, he took a breather and sat on a bench. A scruffy gentleman came and sat down beside him and said, "You know, life is a hyphen." Jepson just sort of shrugged his youthful shoulders and said, "Yeah." Then he looked at the tombstones and he realized what his new friend was saying as he saw that all the tombstones had one thing in common: a date—a hyphen—and then another date. Then the disheveled, very wise man got up and said, "Make the most of it young man. Life is a hyphen."

Jepson says, "We know when our starting date is, but we don't know what the ending date is, and the trick is to extend that hyphen as long as we can. If you're really clever, you can extend it beyond the end date." Jepson will certainly be long remembered and respected for many contributions, but the Jepson School of Leadership at the University of Richmond ensures his legacy. He says, "You try to leave something behind that will make the world a better place and in some way help others along their paths, and hopefully they will do the same." RMITs pay it forward.

Salt Lake City, Utah's Jon Huntsman says, "Selfless giving unto others represents one's true wealth." This quote is inscribed proudly on the Huntsman Cancer Institute in Salt Lake City. Huntsman has certainly been selfless in his giving. He has already bestowed three-quarters of a billion dollars on the Huntsman Institute, which is based at the University of Utah. Upon completion of the sale of his company, which is expected to garner more than $10 billion, he will be even more selfless. Huntsman is committed; he has survived cancer three times.

Dayton's Clay Mathile earmarked more than $100 million to give to his employees when he sold Iams to Procter and Gamble; he endowed a community fund for the Dayton area with another $100 million. The sale of his company benefited everyone associated with it—his family, his employees, and his community. That's what you call the ultimate win–win. Jorge Pérez says, "What I'm concerned about right now is not my success, but rather my legacy."

Inheritance Is Inherently Bad

What might surprise you is that the majority of RMITs don't plan to leave most of their money to their kids and grandkids when they are called to a higher position. David Green says, "I don't want any of my family to get anything they didn't earn. I look at Hobby Lobby as a tree in nature—a tree that no one really owns, but because we have tended the tree, we get the fruits for caring for it. I have gotten the fruits of what I have earned; whoever follows me should only get the fruits of what they earn." Warren Buffett still believes today, as he did in 1986 when he first said it, that "a very rich person should leave his kids enough to do anything, but not enough to do nothing."

There are many ways to give back to the universe. Bill Kellogg, the main man of Milwaukee and the former CEO of Kohl's, now enjoys investing in people and businesses that interest him—that is one way he feels he can give back to society. He, like most RMITs, has failed miserably at retirement, but that's a failure he can live with. After a lifetime of working twelve-hour days, seven days a week, rest is not high on Kellogg's or any RMIT's priority list. RMITs don't retire; they refocus, they regenerate, and they never stop questing for the next big thing and the best way in which to make a personal difference.

During the building of his Harco pharmacy fortune, Jim Harrison of Tuscaloosa was famous for saying, "When we get some money, we're going to do some good." When he sold Harco to Rite Aid, he got some money all right. Now he is doing some major good through the Harrison Family Foundation. "Running the foundation and giving away money is the greatest joy of my life," he says. One of the greatest joys of Jim Click's life (other than selling another car or truck) is helping people with disabilities. He believes in making a difference while you're around to see that difference being made. He currently employs more than seventy people with disabilities. Christel DeHaan of Indianapolis is using the same skills that helped her build RCI into an $825 million payday to build and run Christel House International. Her hope is to break the cycle of poverty with learning centers in Mexico, Venezuela, India, South Africa, and the United States.

Bob Stiller's Green Mountain Coffee has been successful in more than just the financial sense. His company has found ways to be socially responsible. It gives 5 percent of pretax profits each year to various social and environmental initiatives; it pays employees for one hour of volunteer work a week; it even offers meditation training. It is not surprising, then, that Green Mountain has been named one of the most socially responsible companies in America by *Business Ethics* magazine. Stiller has proved that you can do well (make loads of money) and do good simultaneously. He has imbued his employees with his same sense of social responsibility. He knows how to give and why. RMITs know that from whom much is given, much is expected.

PERSONAL PROFILES OF THE RICHEST MEN IN TOWN

Akron, OH: James Oelschlager

Founder and CEO of Oak Associates, Ltd., an investment management and mutual funds company with more than $30 billion under management. Despite the effects of multiple sclerosis, Oelschlager has become one of the nation's most respected investors. He began his career working for Firestone Tire and Rubber Company managing a pension fund before deciding the only way to make his fortune was to strike out on his own. Firestone became his first client. His wife, Vanita, wrote a book called *Jimisms*. My favorite: "I would like to say to those people with multiple sclerosis: Don't let MS be an excuse." Not surprisingly, he says, "There is no one I would want to change places with. I want to be me." Oelschlager holds a BA in economics from Denison University and a JD from Northwestern University School of Law.

Albany, NY: Guha and Karthik Bala

The brother–brother team that founded the video gaming company Vicarious Visions, the creator of video and computer games like Tony Hawk's Downhill Jam, Spider-man 3, Shrek the Third, and Nintendo's Guitar Hero III. The CEO and president, respectively, started the company in their parents' basement in the early 1990s while they were still in high school. In 2005, they sold Vicarious Visions to the Activision Blizzard, an $8 billion interactive gaming company that is now the largest in the world. The brothers still run the Vicarious Visions division. Karthik has degrees in computer science and psychology from Rensselaer Polytechnic Institute, and Guha has an honors degree in chemistry from Harvard University.

Amherst, MA: Michael Kittredge

The founder of the Yankee Candle Company, Kittredge started in his mom's kitchen in South Hadley, Massachusetts, at the age of sixteen in an attempt to make her an inexpensive Christmas gift. The rock band that he had hoped would create his fortune had broken up, and he was flat broke. That one candle, made from melted crayons in an old milk container, had within two decades become a $100 million company and the leading scented candle maker in the world. In 1998, when he was forty-five, Kittredge sold 90 percent of his firm to private equity company Fortsman Little and reaped a half-billion-dollar fortune. Today Yankee Candle is a billion-dollar business, and the former candle maker makes his lifestyle fragrant at his homes in Amherst, Nantucket, Florida, and aboard his 200-foot Feadship yacht.

Anchorage, AK: Robert Gillam

President and CEO of McKinley Asset Management, an investment company he founded in 1990. "The Peter Lynch of the Northwest," Gillam grew up in the back-room warehouse of his father's liquor store after his parents' divorce. He made his way to Wharton and UCLA, ultimately becoming not only the richest man in Anchorage but also the richest man in Alaska. He has proven that you can successfully manage money anywhere in the United States and make millions with just a little technology, a lot of smarts—and a hangar full of jets. A true Alaskan adventurer, Gillam says, "Alaska is the Switzerland of America." He loves the wilds of America's forty-ninth state, where he fishes, hunts, skis, hikes, and pilots his own floatplane over three million lakes.

Anderson, CA: Archie "Red" Emmerson

Chairman of Sierra Pacific Industries, a wood products manufacturing company that is the third largest producer of timber in the country. Emmerson is also either the largest or the second largest landowner in the United States, owning well over a million acres, competing with Ted Turner. "I think Ted has a couple more acres," he admits. He believes you can never own too much land or learn too much from other successful people. He says, "I love to read biographies of successful people—people that I respect. I have never subscribed to the *Wall Street Journal.*"

Atlanta, GA: Bernard Marcus

With his partner, Arthur Blank, Marcus founded the Home Depot in 1979 after being fired from Handy Dan—a home improvement retailer that Home Depot ultimately put out of business. Revenge is sweet, but that's not how Marcus sees it today. He says, "Getting fired was the best thing that ever happened to me." The Home Depot is the largest and most successful home improvement company in the world. In just twenty-eight years, the company grew from three stores to more than two thousand, and from two hundred employees to more than three hundred thousand of what the Home Depot calls associates, thanks to Marcus. Marcus's billions have allowed him to become Atlanta's most prominent philanthropist. He is the man and the money

($200 million) behind the Georgia Aquarium, the largest aquarium in the world, which opened in 2005.

Austin, TX: Michael Dell

Founder and CEO of Dell, Inc., Michael laid the groundwork for his eponymous company in 1984 in his dorm room at the University of Texas. He dropped out of college to pursue his dream of building the world's most successful computer company, by eliminating the middleman. The word *direct* is today firmly associated with only one computer company. A mere fourteen years after his dorm room dream, Dell, Inc. had become the second largest manufacturer of computers in the world. Today Michael Dell is worth $17 billion and is back in the CEO's seat after a stint as the company's chairman. It seems no one can run the company as successfully as the man with the original vision— and the one who has the most at stake.

Baltimore, MD: Stephen Bisciotti

The elusive billionaire owner and CEO of the Baltimore Ravens, Bisciotti (pronounced *bih-SHAH-tee*) is the second youngest owner of an NFL team. He also co-founded Aerotek (now Allegis Group), a temporary employment company providing employees to the aerospace and technology sectors. Allegis is the third largest staffing firm in the United States and sixth largest in the world, creating the majority of his billion-dollar fortune.

Bangor, ME: Stephen King

The king of horror novels often referred to as America's best loved bogeyman is one of the richest writers in American history. He graduated from the University of Maine at Orono in 1970 with a BA in English and few prospects of finding a teaching job. He became a laborer at an industrial laundry, but supplemented his meager income with the occasional sale of a short story. King's breakthrough novel, *Carrie*, catapulted him to literary stardom. *Carrie* sold millions of copies and led to seventy-five more King books at last count, making him one of the most prolific authors in America. His books have spawned dozens of Hollywood hit movies.

Belspring, Virginia: Randal J. "RJ" Kirk

Biotech billionaire, air force brat, University of Virginia Law graduate, Kirk is the fast-moving, faster-talking founder of GIV (General Injectibles and Vaccines). He also founded New River Pharmaceuticals, which pioneered the development of the breakthrough ADHD drug Vyvanse. In 2005, Kirk sold New River Pharmaceuticals to Shire, the maker of Adderall, for $2.6 billion. He is currently senior managing director and chief executive officer of Third Security, LLC, a life sciences venture capital and private equity company that he founded in 1999. Kirk also serves as chairman of the board of Clinical Data, Inc. (NASDAQ: CLDA), and serves on the board of directors of Halozyme Therapeutics, Inc. (NASDAQ: HALO).

Birmingham, AL: Miller Gorrie

The Southern construction czar who owns one of the largest privately held companies in the United States. Gorrie purchased the small construction company in 1964 with the proceeds from his early investment in IBM stock (which he'd bought in the 1950s with the money he earned from his paper route) and from summer construction jobs. He says, "By 1960, I had over $100,000 in IBM stock because the growth stock had been growing by 20 to 25 percent per year." The Auburn University engineering graduate spent three years in the US Navy's Civil Engineering Corps after college before purchasing the small Thomas C. Brasfield construction company, which he later renamed Brasfield and Gorrie, even though the previous owner had no affiliation with his company. Gorrie's company has poured the concrete for the Georgia Dome and Georgia Aquarium, and has more than $2 billion of annual construction revenue.

Boston, MA: Peter M. Nicholas

Co-founder (with John Abele) of Boston Scientific, a medical products company that changed the way surgery is done around the world. The Duke University and Wharton graduate is non-executive chairman of the firm, which is the leading maker of catheters, stents, and medical devices that allow for less invasive surgery. Under his leadership, Boston Scientific's value has grown to better than $20 billion. He says, "There's a big difference between long-term sustainable success and fast bubble success." His has been the former.

Boulder, CO: Judi Paul

Chairman of Renaissance Learning, Inc. (NASDAQ: RLRN), the reading and math motivation and progress software company whose Accelerated Reader program is now used in sixty-seven thousand schools. Paul first created a quiz-based program to help her own kids learn to love to read and to find success in reading; it's now the nation's leading reading management and progress program. She ran her nascent company in her basement so she could do laundry and take care of four children simultaneously. At her husband, Terry's suggestion, she encouraged a local Wisconsin Rapids, Wisconsin, school to test her accelerated reading program. It met with great success. Renaissance Learning has a market capitalization of more than half a billion dollars.

Buffalo, NY: Robert Wilmers

Chairman and CEO of M&T Bank Corporation. In 1982, Buffalo's half-billion-dollar man purchased First Empire State Corporation, which became M&T Bank. Educated at Phillips

Exeter and Harvard, Wilmers is also involved in the Andy Warhol Foundation for the Visual Arts and the Vivian Beaumont Theatre at Lincoln Center; he's a member of the Harvard University John F. Kennedy School of Government Visiting Committee as well as the Council on Foreign Relations. He and his French-born wife rub shoulders with the fashionable elite at their vineyard Château Haut Bailly in France.

Burlington, VT: Robert Stiller

Founder and chairman of Green Mountain Coffee Roasters, Inc. (NASDAQ: GMCR), which has financially outperformed Howard Schultz's Starbucks over the past decade. Stiller began his entrepreneurial career as co-founder of "cigarette" rolling paper company EZ Wider, which he sold in 1980—reaping a $3 million payday. He then parlayed his win and windfall into becoming the coffee king of the Green Mountains of Vermont. He is not only the most successful man in Vermont, but also possibly the busiest: He owns Heritage Flight, an air charter company; is working on artificial intelligence technology to teach meditation telephonically; and is cleaning up cow manure and processing it in ways that benefit the environment.

Carrollton, GA: Robert J. Stone

The most successful man in my hometown. The former Lockheed Aircraft and Southern Railway software programmer fell in love with computers when he took his first computer course at Georgia Tech. He says, "From the first time I laid my eyes on a computer, I saw it as a device to solve problems—and I love to solve problems." He left the business world to teach business at Georgia State, but it was a new job at West Georgia College (now the University of West Georgia) that brought him to Carrollton. The happy professor reluctantly rejoined the business world when it became apparent that no one else in town knew how to program computers. As a favor to the head of the local Department of Family and Children's Services office, he spent a weekend writing a computer program automating the distribution of food stamps—a process that had previously been done by hand. Stone's innovative software so simplified an otherwise unruly system that news quickly spread. His success allowed him to scale his business to all 159 counties in Georgia. At $1 per transaction, he soon built a $26 million business, scaling his business to twenty states. Today SMI is a thriving $40 million company run by his kids. In addition to his family-owned Systems and Methods Incorporated, Stone has built a real estate development company with his daughter and grandson. They are currently designing, building, and selling residential properties on Lake Wedowee, just across the border in Alabama.

Charlotte, NC: O. Bruton Smith

The auto-racing billionaire who owns Speedway Motorsports, Inc., which includes the Charlotte Motor Speedway, Las Vegas Motor Speedway, and Texas Motor Speedway. He is also chairman and CEO of Sonic Automotive, a company with more than 180 automobile dealerships. Smith is the hyperaggressive salesman who brought NASCAR to Wall Street: Speedway was the first motor-sports company to trade on the New York Stock Exchange. Cars are in his blood. The son of a cotton farmer, Smith dreamed of being a race-car driver as far back as he can recall and bought his first race car at seventeen. He then built his beloved Charlotte Motor Speedway, lost it to bankruptcy, and got it back. From broke to billionaire, Smith's journey has been one of high drama. He loves to sell and he loves to make a splash—he once had Elvis impersonators parachute down to his Charlotte racetrack for a pre-race show.

Chicago, IL: Sam Zell

The $6 billion man and Chicago native who owns Equity Group Investments LLC was once the reigning king of real estate investment trusts and often referred to as the country's largest landlord. Today Zell spends most of his time as a press lord, having acquired the Tribune Company of Chicago, but in true RMIT fashion, he is currently fighting a big battle. The Tribune Company owns some of the most prestigious newspaper and media properties in the country—the *Chicago Tribune*, the *Los Angeles Times*, and the *Baltimore Sun*, not to mention the Chicago Cubs and Wrigley Field. He recently filed for Chapter 11 bankruptcy protection to give him some time to reorganize the company into a leaner and profitable enterprise. He often refers to himself as a "grave dancer," and my bet is he'll once again rise to the challenge. He sold Equity Office Properties to the Blackstone Group for $39 billion after all, which was the largest leveraged buyout in American history at the time. The University of Michigan and University of Michigan Law School graduate says, "I'm a professional opportunist."

Cleveland, OH: A. Malachi Mixon

Chairman and CEO of Invacare, the world's largest manufacturer and distributor of home health care products such as wheelchairs, walkers, and home oxygen systems. Mixon led a management buyout of his company from Johnson and Johnson in 1979, when Invacare had just $19.5 million in sales. Under Mixon's care, it has grown to $1.5 billion in net sales. "Money isn't important," he says, "until you want to buy something." He has recently bought his hometown the Cleveland Institute of Music, a new 250-seat recital hall that bears his name. The longtime Republican is also chairman of the board of trustees of the Cleveland Clinic Foundation, and has established a chair in entrepreneurial studies at the Weatherhead School of Management at Case Western Reserve University.

Cleveland, TN: W. Allan Jones

The CEO and founder of Checks Into Cash, Jones is not just the richest but also by far the most colorful character in his hometown (population thirty-eight thousand) just outside Chattanooga. He founded his subprime loan company in 1993, and today it is the third largest payday lending company in America, boasting $1 billion a year in revenue. Before he attained his payday loan prominence, Jones ran Credit Bureau Services of Cleveland, the largest credit collection agency in Tennessee. He describes himself as "the only person in town with the guts to drive a Bentley and a Maybach." Jones is a hyperdevoted historic preservationist in his hometown, providing the funding for a serious face-lift of downtown Cleveland. He has also preserved the local burger and milk-shake joint—known as "The Spot"—which was established in 1937, and the upscale Bald Headed Bistro that he says is named for himself. "I have always wanted a limestone mansion just like the Beverly Hillbillies," he says. He's got it, except he had to settle for Texas limestone instead of Indiana limestone like the Clampetts' mansion. For his twenty-fifth-anniversary Halloween party, he brought the stars of the 1960s sitcom *Leave It to Beaver*—Jerry Mathers, Tony Dow, and Ken Osmond—to celebrate with him and 25,000 of his friends. When hiring, he says, "I look for people who have their antennae high in the air."

Colorado Springs, CO: Leroy Landhuis

This spirited Bible scholar has created the largest and most successful real estate development and management company in Colorado Springs. The air force NORAD (North American Air Defense Command) veteran has vast real estate operations in the Western states. He is quiet about his money, but vociferous about his faith and his desire to change the world. Landhuis says, "People are drawn to courage." He has had the courage to find the ideal intersection of strong faith in God and capitalism. Today his companies—The Landhuis Company of Colorado and Paradigm Realty Advisors of Tulsa, Oklahoma—manage and account for hundreds of thousands of square feet of office and commercial space as well as thousands of acres of developable land. Landhuis wants his Pikes Peak development to give first-time buyers access to the American Dream. While real estate has given him his great wealth, he says that God has given him the real meaning in life.

Columbia, SC: Joe E. Taylor

The former CEO of Southland Log Homes, Taylor is today the secretary of commerce for the state of South Carolina and also a part-time venture capitalist. His principal responsibility is to attract to his home state information- and technology-based businesses that will increase income levels and enhance South Carolinians' quality of life. Taylor became president and chief executive officer of Southland Log Homes before he was twenty-five years old, and built the company into the largest producer of pre-cut log homes in the world. In 2004, Taylor sold Southland to a private equity company, Arcapita Inc., but he continues to serve on the board of directors. His passionate mission today is to encourage more local companies to build their businesses and remain happily ever after in the Palmetto State.

Columbus, OH: Leslie H. Wexner

The founder of the Limited Inc.—the company behind Victoria's Secret—is in touch with his feminine side. His net worth of at least $3 billion is not Victoria's secret, or anyone else's for that matter. He also owns Bath & Body Works and New York's Fifth Avenue retailer Henri Bendel. The highly secretive CEO doesn't allow calls to his office from the company's main line. His penchant for the finer things in life, however, is not so secret. He lives in a $50 million Georgian mansion in New Albany, Ohio, has luxury homes in Palm Beach and Aspen, and owns one of the world's largest yachts—appropriately named the *Limitless*.

Dallas, TX: Harold C. Simmons

Worth a reported $7 billion, this press-shy, highly controversial corporate raider is chairman of Valhi, his holding company, valued at more than $3 billion. The banker-turned-pharmacy-owner-turned-pharmacy-chain-owner (before he sold to Eckerd) has been at the center of bankruptcies, bad deals, bad bonds, and bad blood in his family, but the investor and conglomerate builder always seems to come out smelling like the yellow rose of his Texas. This poor boy from Golden, Texas, who grew up in a house with no running water, signed a 1989 letter to *Fortune*, "Harold C. Simmons, M.A. Economics, Phi Beta Kappa, Billionaire." He told the magazine, "I only know how to do one thing well and that's read a financial statement." I met him at the home of Nancy Hamon, the richest woman in Dallas, but I could not wangle a personal interview, even after numerous letters and more than thirty phone calls. Simmons proves that when you're the richest man in town, you can make the rules, and he does.

Danbury, CT: Fred DeLuca

The submarine sandwich sultan founded his company with a $1,000 loan from family friend Dr. Peter Buck. Privately held Subway today has approximately twenty-nine thousand stores and has made both DeLuca and Buck billionaires. As the leader of the largest fast-food franchise company in the world, DeLuca is known as a masterful marketing expert. Witness the "Jared" commercial that made his sub shop franchises a place to turn for fast-food weight loss. He says, "I'm not a natural persuader. I'm no Barack Obama." Yet he has persuaded twenty-nine thousand entrepreneurs to join his Subway team as franchisees.

Dayton, OH: Clayton H. Mathile

The former owner and CEO of Iams, the premium pet foods company he sold to Procter and Gamble for $2.3 billion in 1999. Mathile (pronounced *ma-TEEL*) is passionate about education and has founded the Center for Entrepreneurial Education just outside his hometown. He realized early on in the development of Iams that the most important thing he could do was hire dog and cat lovers. Those animal people helped him build a company from near scratch into a multibillion-dollar success. He knew from an early age that he wanted to be an entrepreneur and own his own business. He says, "I have always liked my own version of Goethe's declaration, 'Dream no little dreams, for they have no magic to move men's souls.'" This inspired him to title his book about his life and business experiences *Dream No Little Dreams*. He has dreamed only big dreams.

Daytona Beach, FL: Ron Rice

Founder of Hawaiian Tropic. The suntan lotion salesman and master marketer created his first lotion concoction in garbage cans and sold his product directly from his lifeguard station on the beaches of Florida. Rice pioneered the Miss Hawaiian Tropic beauty contest as a way to build the Hawaiian Tropic brand. He sold his company in August 2007 to Playtex for a reported $83 million. He started out his career as a teacher and a coach. While he loved both, they didn't love him back. "I taught for eight years at seven schools and was fired six times," he says. "My failures taught me my greatest lessons—the most important thing I learned in life was that when I fell down, I could get back up."

Denver, CO: Charles W. Ergen

Co-founder, chairman, and CEO of EchoStar Communications, Inc., and the DISH Network (NASDAQ GS: DISH), the satellite TV folks. Worth more than $10 billion, Ergen is an ace poker player who bet the farm in 1995 when he launched the first direct-broadcast satellite into orbit on a Chinese rocket. The gamble paid off: In 1980, Ergen and gambling buddy Jim De-Franco, along with Ergen's future wife, scraped together $60,000 and started his satellite dish company. The Ergens and DeFranco purchased a couple of satellite dishes after running the tables in Las Vegas—only to lose them en route to Colorado, when gale-force winds blew them and their dishes off the road. They were able to salvage only one. Still, that dish served them well as their demonstration sample in what was to become a sales frenzy in the mountains of Colorado, where TV signals are weak because of the terrain. Today, EchoStar (DISH) has a market capitalization in excess of $16 billion. Ergen owns more than half of its shares.

Des Moines, IA (Ankeny): Dennis Albaugh

Iowa's chemical king, dubbed the Prince of Pesticides by *Forbes* magazine, is the 100 percent owner of his company Albaugh Inc. Living part of the year in Marco Island, Florida, Albaugh has come a long way from his Ankeny, Iowa, farm roots. The billionaire boy wonder started as a fertilizer salesman and then mortgaged his home to buy a truck to haul weed-killing chemicals to a potential customer in South Dakota. Today Albaugh's multibillion-dollar company, although still based in Ankeny, Iowa, has operations as far afield as Brazil and Argentina. He also has all the amenities (his own private golf course, boats, and planes) of the billionaire that he is. Like many RMITs, he is making his hometown of Ankeny a priority by developing real estate there. His current project, Prairie Hill, is a green community that is to be Iowa's largest new urban development.

Detroit, MI: William Davidson

The Motor City glass magnate is chairman of Guardian Industries and enjoys a net worth of $4 billion. His company is the world's largest manufacturer of automotive glass. He satisfies his powerful passion for sports by owning the Detroit Pistons of the NBA, the Detroit Shock of the WNBA, and the Tampa Bay Lightning of the NHL. In 2004, he made sports history by becoming the first owner to win championships in three different professional leagues. Davidson began his career as a lawyer but left the legal profession to breathe new life into Guardian, which at the time had been owned by a relative who had gone bankrupt. Davidson picked up the shattered pieces.

El Paso, TX: William D. Sanders

The regent of real estate investment trusts, Sanders made his first fortune at LaSalle Partners in Chicago, a company he founded in 1968, which became the second largest property manager in the United States. Then he worked his moneymaking magic again with a real estate venture capital company, Security Capital, which he founded in the early 1990s—a time when real estate was in the tank. He took Security public in 1997 and reaped a second fortune. Now the Cornell graduate is changing the landscape of his hometown, El Paso, with his latest venture, Verde Realty. Sanders's business role model was Tom Watson of IBM. In his career, he has hired more than a hundred IBM professionals because of the buttondown, people-first culture and strategic training IBMers enjoyed. This people-first philosophy has led Jeff Allen—a former employee of Security Capital who now owns his own firm, J. B. Allen Realty in San Juan Capistrano, California—to say, "Bill put together a team of the most highly talented people in the real estate industry ever under one roof." He's still doing it today, just back home in El Paso instead of Chicago.

Fargo, ND: Gary Tharaldson

The former North Dakota farm boy is now a hotel king who operates more than 350 hotel properties bearing the names Residence Inn by Marriott, Courtyard by Marriott, Hampton Inn by Hilton, Holiday Inn Express, and Comfort Inn. Tharaldson owns and runs the largest independent hotel property management company in the United States, and is currently developing properties in Las Vegas. In March 2006, the Tharaldson family sold 130 hotels to the Whitehall Real Estate Fund (a division of Goldman Sachs) for a reported $1.2 billion in cash. He says, "I have always outworked everybody else." With his billion in the bank today, he doesn't have to anymore, but he does anyway—as with so many RMITs, it's who he is. It's what he loves.

Fisher Island, FL, and Troy, MI: Bharat Desai

The co-founder and CEO of Syntel (NASDAQ: SYNT), a multibillion-dollar information technology company headquartered in Troy, Michigan. Along with his wife, Neerja Sethi, Desai started Syntel while both were in graduate school at the University of Michigan. The Kenyan-born, Indian-educated Desai was one of the early technology outsourcing leaders. The Desais live in ultra-exclusive Fisher Island, Florida, when they are not in India at Syntel's offices in Mumbai or building the new eighteen-hundred-acre Syntel campus in Pune, India. "Globalization is an irreversible mega-trend," Desai says, "and America should actively promote globalization." Syntel competes with IBM, EDS, and Accenture, but he says, "Companies prefer to work with us because we are a nimble, hungry, and responsible company."

Fort Lauderdale, FL: Wayne Huizenga

America's most serious serial entrepreneur, the former trash hauler has hauled in a $3 billion fortune by building three Fortune 1000 companies: Waste Management, Blockbuster, and

AutoNation. He has been a partner behind Extended Stay America and has the distinction of being the only man to own three major-league sports franchises at one time: the Miami Dolphins, Florida Marlins, and Florida Panthers.

Fort Worth, TX: David Bonderman

The private equity potentate of Texas Pacific Group (TPG), which has made major investments in J. Crew, Neiman Marcus, Burger King, Bally's, Ducati, Continental Airlines, and TXU. The Harvard Law graduate, who was once a major deal strategist for Texas billionaire Robert Bass, has more than $30 billion of assets under management at TPG, which he founded in 1992. "Bondo," as he is often called, learned at the knee of famed investor Richard Rainwater while he was managing the big Bass money. Rainwater still calls Fort Worth home and is most likely slightly richer than Bonderman, but he spends much of his time with wife Darla Moore in their Lake City, South Carolina, home. Like most private equity privateers, Bonderman was reluctant to be interviewed. He finally relented, but not easily. He said in an e-mail, "I'm prepared to listen, not sure I'm prepared to talk." He did talk, but said little. His success, though, speaks for itself.

Fresno, CA: David McDonald

Patriot prince of Pelco, the security and surveillance systems company that McDonald bought in the early 1980s, built into an international company, and sold for $1.7 billion in 2007, to French conglomerate Schneider Electric. He remains chairman of the board. If you have ever felt as though you're being watched, you were most likely being sized up by Pelco's security systems, which currently protect the queen of England at Buckingham Palace, the Statue of Liberty, and the Presidential Palace in China. The California company honored New York's police officers and firefighters by bringing many of them to its Clovis headquarters on September 11, 2002, one year after the tragedy, to thank them personally. To signal its patriotism and honor all those who died on that sad day, the company constructed a 9/11 memorial at its headquarters as well.

Grand Rapids, MI: Richard DeVos

The multilevel selling magnate who founded Amway with high school best friend Jay Van Andel has built a multibillion-dollar privately held company and a multibillion-dollar fortune. The ultimate optimist has written three books, *Believe!*, *Compassionate Capitalism*, and *Hope From My Heart: Ten Lessons for Life*. The devoted family man and ardent Republican owns the NBA's Orlando Magic.

Greenville, SC: Leighton Cubbage

The former Clemson University linebacker and communications entrepreneur has built more than thirty companies since graduating in 1976. Cubbage made his first fortune when he sold Corporate Telemanagement Group. He has served as chairman of New South Communications, chief executive officer of telecommunications firm iOnosphere Inc., and chairman of Rhino Automotive; he is a principal investor in the Greenville Rhinos Arena Football League team.

Greenwich, CT: Thomas Peterffy

The founder and CEO of Interactive Brokers (NASDAQ: IBKR) grew up in communist Hungary and came to the United States originally to work as an engineering draftsman . . . until he had the opportunity to program a computer. Though he spoke no English, he spoke the language of software. Peterffy says his background in computer programming is what most influences his approach to business today. He founded Interactive Brokers in 1977, and is today almost twice as rich ($11 billion) as his neighbor, the much more publicized Greenwich hedge fund honcho Steve Cohen (worth an estimated $6 billion). Cohen, as the CEO of SAC Capital Advisors, has a penchant for making big money, building big houses, and buying big art. Peterffy prefers to be much quieter. His Interactive Brokers, including his market-making unit Timber Hill, executes more than two million equity-based option contracts worldwide every day. It's anything but quiet.

Harrisburg, PA: Alex Hartzler

A triathlon-running, house-renovating, tech-savvy master networker and real estate developer, Hartzler founded the Harrisburg Young Professionals (HYP). He made his first fortune on the sale of Webclients, a company that ran Web sites focused on generating leads for advertisers, which he and partners Josh Gray and Scott Piotroski sold to ValueClick in 2005 for $141 million. He is currently president of WCI Partners, a real estate development company that he founded in 2005 to make downtown Harrisburg more historically beautiful and his bank account more bountiful. His favorite quote about business and success is Thomas Edison's "Vision without execution is hallucination," which he attributes to his former partner Josh Gray.

Hartford, CT: Ronald Williams

The chairman and CEO of Aetna, the health care benefits company, is a Roosevelt University and MIT graduate. Williams got his big start in the health insurance business at Blue Cross of California. He also sits on the board of his friend Ken Chenault's American Express Corporation. Williams joined Aetna in 2001, when the company was in deep financial crisis. He effected a major turnaround employing a balance of informational technology and leadership skills. His big claim to fame was instituting the Executive Management Information System (EMIS)—a data system that gathered information from across all the business units, yielding a whole new approach to performance measures. He is considered a charismatic leader with superior people skills. He has said, "When you ask people to do what is considered undoable, you have to work with them, coach them, and remove barriers, but it all starts with the belief that people want to do the right things."

Hollis, NH: Patrick McGovern

The founder and CEO of IDG, the largest technology publishing, research, and event management company in the world. While still a student at MIT, McGovern began his career in publishing by working for the first US computer magazine, *Computers and Automation*. In this first job, he learned his biggest business lesson from Tom Watson: Listen to your customer's needs and meet them. He founded IDG as a research company to provide information to the computer industry with only $5,000 he received from the sale of his car. He was able to persuade the major computer companies, including IBM, to pay 50 percent up front for the research he would eventually deliver.

The company has grown to more than $3 billion in revenue derived from publishing more than three hundred magazines, including its flagship, *Computerworld*. IDG produces more than 750 events and expos in fifty-five countries, including the international series of LinuxWorld Conference & Expo and Macworld Conference & Expo. McGovern is also a trustee of his alma mater, MIT, where he has funded the McGovern Institute for Brain Research, which is studying the neurogenesis of the brain.

Honolulu, HI: Jay H. Shidler

The serial entrepreneur, founder, and owner of The Shidler Group, the largest real estate development company in Hawaii, which owns more than 10 percent of Honolulu's office space. He purchased his first building, the Polynesian Plaza in Hawaii, in 1972, followed by acquisitions in Santa Barbara and Seattle. By the late 1980s, The Shidler Group had twelve offices on the mainland, including San Francisco, Los Angeles, Chicago, and New York City. Today Shidler's company owns more than two thousand properties across the country and in Canada and over 1.5 million square feet of office space. He has also founded four companies listed on the New York Stock Exchange: TriNet Corporate Realty Trust, Inc. (now called iStar Financial, Inc.; NYSE: SFI), First Industrial Realty Trust, Inc. (NYSE: FR), Corporate Office Properties Trust (NYSE: OFC), and Primus Guaranty, Ltd. (NYSE: PRS). Hawaii's main man recently gave the University of Hawaii its largest gift ever to create the Shidler School of Business.

Houston, TX: Dan Duncan

The co-founder and chairman of Enterprise Products Partners. EPCO is a New York Stock Exchange company with a market capitalization of over $13 billion, giving Duncan a conservative net worth of more than $8 billion. The onetime postal worker and big-game hunter says, "True wealth is really measured in the lives you touch, not the dollars you have."

Indianapolis, IN: Christel DeHaan

The co-founder and former chairman of Resort Condominiums International, the largest vacation exchange company in the world. (Many folks right outside Indianapolis think that Mel Simon, the Brooklyn-born multibillionaire and shopping center shogun, is Indianapolis's RMIT. Simon, however—who also owns pro basketball's Indiana Pacers—lives today in Palm Beach.) Christel DeHaan is often referred to in travel circles as the time-share queen. The former governess who first ran a typing service in her home in Indianapolis ultimately built RCI into a company that she was able to sell to Henry Silverman's Cendant Corporation for $825 million in 1996. She has since devoted her life to helping children in developing countries through her Christel House International program.

The Christel House mission is to break the cycle of poverty by educating young people in Mexico, Venezuela, India, and South Africa, helping them to become self-sufficient. In the spirit of the Chinese proverb "Give a man a fish and you feed him for a day; teach a man to fish and you feed him for a lifetime," DeHaan says, "We teach young people how to fish—how to navigate their world in a way that breaks the cycle of poverty. We teach them practical life skills, and we teach them character." Her twenty-six hundred children receive the help and guidance they need to achieve productive, self-sufficient lives. DeHaan is using the same business principles with Christel House International that she used so successfully in the for-profit world with Resort Condominiums International: She believes in metrics, accountability, and transparency.

Kansas City, KS: Min Kao

Co-founder and CEO of Garmin Corporation, the world's largest producer of global positioning systems. The GPS guru is a native of Taiwan who came to the United States to pursue his education at the University of Tennessee. He became a systems analyst for Teledyne and worked with the US Army before using his software development expertise to found Garmin in 1989. Today it's a $4.5 billion international company, giving Min Kao a personal fortune valued at more than $3 billion.

Kansas City, MO: James E. Stowers

The founder of mutual fund company American Century Funds, with more than $100 billion under management. In

1958, medical school dropout and former World War II fighter pilot Stowers invested $2,500 of his own money to launch the Twentieth Century Fund, a no-load mutual fund that is still a core component of the mutual fund giant today. He'd learned the investment game as a mutual fund salesman for Waddell and Reed. His fortune-creating epiphany came when he realized that a computer program could change the ways stocks are selected. A cancer survivor, he and his wife founded a multibillion-dollar biomedical research facility called the Stowers Institute for Medical Research.

Knoxville, TN: James A. Haslam II

The owner of privately held Pilot Travel Centers, LLC, and Pilot Corporation. Often called Trucker's Paradise, Pilot is the nation's largest operator of travel centers and largest seller of over-the-road diesel fuel. It all started with just one gas station that Haslam bought shortly after his service in the army at age twenty-seven. The reserved and humble Haslam says he has used the lessons he learned playing football at the University of Tennessee as his tenets for business success. "First you have to get the best players and put them in the right positions, then you have practice, and then you have to execute on Saturdays. The same is true in business, except you have to execute every day and you have to execute with integrity," he says. "The number one value at Pilot is integrity, and that comes first." Today he is executing on philanthropy while still running Pilot. He has made the largest gift ever—$32.5 million—to his alma mater. He says, "You learn, you earn, and then you must give."

Lake Charles, LA: William J. Doré

The high-flying, deep-sea-diving driving force behind Global Industries, a $2 billion marine construction company. At age thirty, he purchased Global Divers and worked hard to become the deep-sea construction leader. He orchestrated more than a dozen major acquisitions with companies much larger than his, including Sea-Con Services, Inc. (a division of Chicago Bridge and Iron Company), in 1987; Santa Fe Offshore Construction Company in 1990; Teledyne Movible Offshore in 1992; the Red Adair Company in 1993; and selected assets and operational bases of SubSea International (a Halliburton company subsidiary) in 1997. Global Industries went public in 1993, applying a well-earned half-billion dollars to Doré's personal balance sheet. He says, "I'm proud of my scorecard." Seven hundred million is indeed something of which to be proud.

Las Vegas, NV: Sheldon Adelson

Las Vegas's biggest gambler grew up on the wrong side of the tracks in Boston as the son of an immigrant taxi driver. He loves to say, "If you don't have a conviction about what you are doing, you are never going to make it." Today the undisputed king of Las Vegas is making it in both Las Vegas and China's new gambling mecca, Macau. Regarding his competitors in China, he recently told *USA Today*, "We will cannibalize them." He still has the means to do so even though his Sands Corporation took a major stock hit during the recent economic crisis. Adelson once had a $28 billion fortune, making him the third richest American, behind Warren Buffett and Bill Gates. Don't cry for Adelson.

Little Rock, AR: Frank Hickingbotham

The founder of TCBY (This Can't Be Yogurt, later changed to The Country's Best Yogurt) was taking a break from shopping with his wife at Neiman Marcus in Dallas when he tasted what he thought was the best dessert he had ever had. Then in his forties and technically retired after selling a series of companies—most recently Old Tyme Foods—he saw his next wealth-creation mechanism in healthy yogurt. The former high school principal built the company from the ground up and took TCBY public in 1984, reaping a small fortune. In 2000, he sold the company to Capricorn Management, which gave him his second bite of the yogurt. With the proceeds from the sale of TCBY, he then set up his own concern investing in luxury companies. Today he is the backer of high-end automobile dealerships such as Desert European Motorcars, which is the number one Rolls-Royce and Bentley dealership in the world. He also owns VIP Motor Cars Ltd. in Palm Springs, California, which houses Mercedes, BMW, Infiniti, and Maybach dealerships; and Newport European Motorcars Ltd. of Newport Beach, the place where he bought his first Rolls-Royce. Still riding high, he also owns Harley-Davidson dealerships in Arkansas, Oklahoma, and Tennessee.

Livonia, MI: Danny Gilbert

The founder and chairman of privately held Quicken Loans and the owner of the Cleveland Cavaliers. He told *Forbes* magazine, "Statistically it's harder to become an owner of a pro sports team than it is to be a pro athlete." The lifetime lover of sports has an *If you can't be one, own one* philosophy. Gilbert starred in business by turning Quicken Loans into the largest Internet mortgage lender in the United States. *Forbes* once reported that at age twelve, he developed a pizza business in his mom's kitchen and arm-twisted his younger brother into being his delivery boy. A local pizza joint that didn't appreciate the competition alerted the health department, and Gilbert's first company was shut down. Always a maverick, he entered the business world in earnest as a real estate agent while attending law school at Wayne State University. He placed a FOR SALE sign on the front lawn of his parents' house—which was definitely not for sale—and used that as a way to gain new customers to whom he would show other houses. He said, "You learn something about mortgages doing that. Not to mention salesmanship." Gilbert recently launched BizdomU, an entrepreneurial boot camp in Detroit designed to train and mentor young entrepreneurs. The goal is to help create jobs and wealth in inner cities.

Los Angeles, CA: Kirk Kerkorian

At ninety, Kerkorian is still making business waves and waves of money with his activist investments. When Kerkorian's holding company, Tracinda Corporation, calls, CEOs begin to quake in their boots. Just ask Ford, Chrysler, or General Motors, or witness his activism at TWA, back in the day.

This $16 billion man made his big fortune in Las Vegas, where he's known as the father of the mega-resort. His most famous property was the MGM Grand Hotel, which he opened in 1973, today known as Bally's. At the time, it was the largest hotel in the world. A high school dropout and former newspaper boy, professional boxer, and Royal Canadian Air Force pilot, he not surprisingly got his real start in the airline business. As a licensed pilot, Kerkorian invested in what he knew. He bought a small air charter business that he renamed Trans International Airlines, ultimately selling it to TWA in 1968 for an $85 million windfall. Two decades later, he would own TWA.

Louisville, KY: David A. Jones Sr.

The co-founder and former chairman of Humana, the well-known managed health care business. Founded with friend Wendell Cherry in 1961 with a $5,000 loan from Household Finance, and a lot of sweat equity, the company began with one nursing home in Louisville. The former accountant and college professor expanded the company (then known as Extendicare) rapidly by building and acquiring more nursing homes. By 1969, he owned the largest nursing home company in the country.

Jones took the company public in 1968. By 1974, he had sold most of the nursing homes in order to acquire hospitals, and by the late 1970s, Humana had become the largest for-profit hospital system in the United States. It established a health insurance division in early 1984 and a decade later spun off the hospitals to its shareholders as an entity called Galen Health Care, Inc., which was sold to Nashville RMIT Tom Frist's HCA. Humana became a health benefits company. This began the modern managed care movement. By the time Jones stepped down as chairman in 2005, Humana was a $20 billion company.

Madison, WI: Pleasant Rowland

Creator of American Girl dolls, which she sold to Mattel for $700 million in 1998. Using a a portion of her doll company fortune, Rowland, like Kim Basinger, purchased a town—Aurora, New York, the home of her alma mater, Wells College. Aurora citizens have been atwitter over her strong my-way-or-the-highway approach to getting things done, but the aging town and college campus are gentrified today thanks to Rowland's millions and dogged determination. She even bought local home furnishings company MacKenzie-Childs out of bankruptcy to save hundreds of jobs. That doesn't mean the locals are happy, however. One resident says, "Pleasant isn't," proving the maxim that no good deed goes unpunished. Today Rowland is spending less time, and much less money, on the town and college she had hoped her fortune would save. Perhaps Aurora, New York's loss will be Madison, Wisconsin's pleasant gain.

Memphis, TN: Frederick W. Smith

The founder, chairman, and CEO of Federal Express wrote a business plan for an overnight delivery company while at Yale University, but his professor thought it was a silly idea. Today, Smith says, "We are the clipper ships of the computer age." FedEx is a $16 billion company, giving Smith a net worth in excess of $2 billion. His philosophy is PSP: People, Service, Profit.

The founding father of the overnight delivery business loves to say of his FedEx idea, "Well the US Postal Service didn't think of it."

Meridian, MS: Hartley Peavey

The founder and CEO of Peavey Electronics, he got his start making guitar amplifiers after coming to the realization that he was not a gifted enough musician to be the next Chuck Berry or Keith Richards. He was, however, good at building things. He found the perfect marriage of his passion, rock music, and his natural talent for engineering and building electronic musical instruments and amplification. Today Peavey has more than two thousand items in its product line, including microphones, mixers, loudspeakers, guitars, power amps, and computer-controlled audio processors. He still loves strumming the guitar, but he much prefers making money from selling his products. Peavey has as many Mississippi maxims as he does millions. He believes the ten most common reasons for failure start with "failure to focus"—and then he lists failure to focus nine more times. He sums up his wealth-creation philosophy with, "If you chase two rabbits, both will escape."

Miami, FL: Jorge Pérez

Known as the Condo Kaiser, Pérez is the driving force behind Miami's Related Group of Florida. He runs the largest Hispanic-owned business in America and one of the largest real estate development companies in the world. Worth several billion dollars, Pérez is partners with fellow University of Michigan graduate Stephen M. Ross, who runs The Related Group New York. The oldest son of Cuban-exile parents, Pérez grew up in Argentina and Bogotá, Colombia, but longed for an American education and the American Dream—and he has achieved both. He says,

"The American Dream is the freedom to do the things you want to do with the people you want to do it with—that's success."

Milwaukee, WI: William Kellogg

The former chairman and CEO of Kohl's Department Stores. Kellogg led a management buyout in 1986 and took the retailer public in 1992, which made him a billionaire. Kellogg built the small Menomonee Falls, Wisconsin–based regional retailer into a major national player, ultimately boasting a market capitalization of more than $13 billion. Currently, he is a venture capital investor with his billion-dollar Kohl's nest egg. He is an investor and director in CarMax, the used-car retailer, among other companies.

Minneapolis, MN: Richard Schulze

The founder of Best Buy, the big-box consumer electronics retailer. Schulze started a modest stereo store called Sound of Music in 1966, which he renamed Best Buy in 1983. Today the reclusive Republican, worth an estimated $4 billion, is spending most of his time teaching at University of St. Thomas's Schulze School of Entrepreneurship, which he has endowed. This is particularly impressive because Schulze never went to college.

Missoula, MT: Dennis Washington

Founder and owner of the Washington Companies, which has investments in multiple companies in heavy construction, mining, transportation, environmental remediation, aviation services, and real estate development. At age twenty-six, he became vice president of the largest construction company in Montana. Before he was thirty, with a loan from a local Caterpillar dealer, Washington began building a company that, by 1969, was the largest contractor in Montana and soon among the largest in the nation. He owns the largest private railroad in the United

States, the largest marine transportation company in Canada, and the Butte Copper Mine. Washington enjoys sailing the high seas aboard his 226-foot yacht, *Attessa*. He can afford to—he's worth $3.5 billion.

Morgantown, WV: Milan "Mike" Puskar

The co-founder, former CEO, and chairman of Mylan Labs, the generic pharmaceutical company that today dispenses more generic drugs than any other company in America. Puskar stepped down from the CEO spot just as the company reached the billion-dollar sales mark. Today Mylan has a market cap of $3.5 billion. Puskar has a net worth in excess of $700 million. He recently gave $20 million to the University of West Virginia, the largest donation in the school's history.

Nashville, TN: Thomas F. Frist Jr.

Co-founder of Hospital Corporation of America (HCA), along with his late father, Thomas Frist Sr., and family friend the late Jack Massey. The former military flight surgeon built HCA into the nation's largest for-profit hospital management company by agglomerating hospitals across the country to take advantage of economies of scale. He's famous for saying, "Banks are together, filling stations are together, grocery stores are together—why can't we put hospitals together? Economy of scale means so much." In 1994, HCA merged with Columbia Health-care, creating even more economies of scale and forming the world's largest hospital company. HCA created a multibillion-dollar fortune for Frist and family.

Newport Beach, CA: Donald Bren

Founder and chairman of the Irvine Company, a massive real estate development firm, Bren almost single-handedly made Orange County, California, into the pristine, über-wealthy retail and technology mecca it has become. He has been the major force behind the development of Newport Beach, the chic, rich town that has more Rolls-Royces per capita than anywhere outside the Middle East. The former marine is a serious snow skier and a significant donor to the Republican party. He's worth $13 billion.

New York, NY: Carl Icahn

The Queens-born activist investor who usually gets his way when he makes a significant investment in a company. He considers himself an "unlocker of inherent value," a capital allocator, and someone who makes things happen. He says, "There are very few companies in American where I couldn't go in and knock 30 percent of cost out of them." Often called a corporate raider—a term Icahn takes umbrage at—Icahn unapologetically insists he invests for one reason only: to make money. He has at least $16 billion to prove it, too. The effect of his investment in a company has come to be called the Icahn Lift, signifying the almost certain stock surge that takes place when he puts his money and influence to work. His mother, a schoolteacher, and his father, a struggling musician and singer, didn't want to pay for his tuition at Princeton, so he worked as a cabana boy at several local beach clubs, sweeping the floors and ultimately sweeping up the cash for his tuition by hard work and even better poker playing. He is famous for saying to the board of Texaco in 1988, "A lot of people die fighting tyranny. The least I can do is vote against it."

Oklahoma City, OK: David Green

Founder and CEO of Hobby Lobby, the arts, crafts, and home decoration superstore company. Green is the son of an Assemblies of God preacher and believes that putting God and family first are the keys to his success. He created a $4 billion fortune from a $600 bank loan. Starting as a stock boy, floor sweeper, and nut roaster for the local five-and-dime in Altus, Oklahoma, Green found his passion in retailing while still in high school. After working for McClellan's 5&10, he became a manager of a local TG&Y, which he says was the Wal-Mart of that era. He saw the opportunity for specialization and started making picture frames on his kitchen table. Sales boomed; two years later, he opened his first Hobby Lobby. Green was never much of an athlete while growing up; he says, "Retail is my sport." His mother and father would have preferred him to join the ministry, but he found his calling in the retail world. He gives God all the credit for his billion-dollar success and has forgone hundreds of millions in profits by not allowing his stores to open on Sundays. "It's the day to be with family and to worship," Green says.

Omaha, NE: J. Joseph Ricketts

We all know that Warren Buffett is Omaha's most famous citizen, and we all know almost everything Buffett has ever uttered about investing and making money. But I was more interested in the wisdom of Omaha's second richest man, Joe Ricketts, the founder and chairman of the board of TD Ameritrade, a discount brokerage that has blossomed thanks to Ricketts's insight into the transformative power of the Internet. "The Internet made me a billionaire," he says. The former commissioned salesperson for brokerage firm Dean Witter always wanted to own his own business, but didn't have the money to make that dream a reality. Being a great salesperson was the next best thing, and was also a way to take control of his destiny. His training in sales eventually led to Ricketts's dream coming true: Today TD Ameritrade enjoys an $11 billion market cap. "TD Ameritrade is humming on all cylinders right now," Ricketts says, so he's turning at least some of his attention to riding motorcycles and thinking about the next big thing.

Orlando, FL: Harris Rosen

This Cornell University graduate has become the most prominent hotel and resort magnate in central Florida. Rosen got his start in the hospitality industry at the famed Waldorf-Astoria Hotel in New York and at various Hilton Hotels, but it was Disney Resorts that brought him to Orlando. Rosen had always dreamed of owning his own hotel. In 1974, that dream came true when he bought the Quality Inn on Orlando's International Drive, which became the basis of an empire that now includes seven successful hotels in the Orlando area. His most recent resort and biggest development yet is Shingle Creek, a 230-acre, fifteen-hundred-room luxury resort and convention center positioned at the headwaters of the Florida Everglades.

Palo Alto, CA: Sergey Brin

Larry Page's Stanford University buddy and the co-founder of Google is worth at least $19 billion. The Google story is perhaps the greatest business success story of the last two decades. Moscow-born Brin is the creator of the Google mission statement, "Do no evil." The son of Russian Jewish parents, he proves the theory that math wizards rule the world. His father is a math professor at the University of Maryland, and his mother is a research scientist at NASA's Goddard Space Flight Center—and according to the best-selling book *The Google Story*, his mother still wants him to complete his graduate degree. Most recently, Brin has plopped down $5 million to reserve a seat on a future private space flight to the International Space Station with Space Adventures, the space tourism company.

Pensacola, FL: Fredric Levin

The king of torts, Levin has been hailed as one of the most successful civil litigation attorneys in the country. He has received more than twenty-five jury verdicts in excess of $1 million (six in excess of $10 million). When not in court, he has even managed the careers of many champion boxers. In 1995, he was selected as National Boxing Manager of the Year while managing Roy Jones Jr. In 1998, he made the largest cash donation ever given to a public law school—his alma mater, the University of Florida School of Law, now called the Fredric G. Levin College of Law. When asked about his greatest accomplishment, however, Levin stated he is most proud of rewriting the Florida Medicaid Third Party Recovery Act, which permits the State of Florida to sue the tobacco industry to recover expenditures for treating illnesses caused by cigarette smoking. He wrote the legislation and was instrumental in its passage. The law has been described as "the single biggest blow against the tobacco industry in United States history." The legislation eventually resulted in a $13 billion settlement for the State of Florida.

Philadelphia, PA: Josh Kopelman

The founder of Infonautics, Half.com, Turn Tide, and First Round Capital—and he's still in his thirties. Kopelman's big windfall came in 2000, when he sold Half.com—the marketplace that connected buyers and sellers of used books, movies, and music—to eBay for $350 million. He has since founded First Round Capital, a seed-stage venture capital fund, making him an investor, director, and adviser to an assortment of technology businesses that he describes as Web 2.0 companies. He writes a tech blog called Red Eye VC. While he's not physically in the Silicon Valley, he is truly at the heart of the new technology revolution.

Portland, ME: Roxanne Quimby

The co-founder of Burt's Bees, an environmentally friendly consumer products company, Quimby saw an opportunity to make candles from the beeswax by-product of boyfriend Burt

Savitz's small-town honey operation. This led to making the lip balm that is still Burt's Bees' best-selling product. In 1993, Roxanne bought out Burt, and eleven years later she sold 80 percent of the company to private equity company AEA, retaining a 20 percent share and a seat on the board. In 2007, Burt's Bees was sold to Clorox for $925 million. An avowed environmentalist, Quimby still maintains a big role in nature conservancy through her Quimby Family Foundation. The foundation's mission is to establish significant areas of wilderness in the state of Maine and to protect those lands for the enjoyment of future generations. Quimby also envisions equal accessibility for Maine residents to the arts in all forms. Quimby now lives part of the year in Palm Beach, where she drives her old pickup truck to fetch her mail. She says, "Why get rid of something that works even if it has three hundred thousand miles on it? I'm too cheap to do that."

Portland, OR: Phillip Knight

The founder and chairman of Nike. The accountant-turned-marketing guru behind the "Just Do It!" campaign—one of the most effective advertising campaigns in history—is a former track star at the University of Oregon who was never satisfied with the quality of running shoes. He believed that better shoes could create better running performance. His coach, Bill Bowerman, the most influential person in his business life, had experimented with his wife's waffle iron to make advanced running shoes, and Knight saw the opportunity to improve the sport with better shoes. After a year stint in the army, Knight went to Stanford Business School and, according to the Stanford alumni magazine, had his aha moment when his professor described the characteristics of an entrepreneur and he said, "That's me." He and Bowerman founded Blue Ribbon Sports, which would later become Nike. The Nike swoosh has given Knight a net worth of $10 billion. After stepping down from the CEO spot in 2005, Knight has found time to go back to school at Stanford University. He most likely pays no tuition for his audited courses, since he has given the Stanford Graduate School of Business a $105 million donation, the largest in the school's history.

Providence, RI: Jonathan Nelson

Nelson is the founder and CEO of Providence Equity Partners, Inc., the private equity powerhouse that currently owns movie studio MGM; sports channels Yankees Entertainment and Sports Network, Inc.; and Hulu, an online-video-on-demand service providing streaming video of TV shows and movies right to your computer. He recently completed the largest leveraged buyout in history, purchasing Bell Canada for $50 billion. The Brown University graduate and Harvard MBA is known for his low-key style and big media turnarounds. His company has turned around and made huge profits on Western Wireless (now AllTell) and Voice Stream Wireless Corporation—which became T-Mobile and was sold to Deutsche Telekom for $24 billion. Nelson learned at Brown University how to find his perfect pitch. He certainly has.

Raleigh, NC: O. Temple Sloan Jr.

The founder and chairman of General Parts, Inc., the nation's third largest automotive parts company, which is also the largest privately held company in North Carolina. Worth $2.5 billion, it's one of the firms that Wall Street investment banks can't wait to get their hooks into. They can hold on to those hooks, though—Duke graduate Sloan has no plans to go public. He's a private man and likes running a private company, though his employees are owners as well through an employee stock option program. He's also the big man on the boards of Bank of America and the Lowe's Companies, Inc.

Rochester, NY: Thomas Golisano

Founder of payroll processing company Paychex, the source of the billion-dollar fortune that allowed him to run for governor of New York three times: in 1994, 1998, and 2002, on the Independent Party ticket. Golisano also owns the NHL team Buffalo Sabres and the Buffalo Bandits lacrosse team and runs the Golisano Foundation, which invests most of its money in Rochester and northwestern New York colleges and charitable causes. Thanks to a $14 million donation, the SUNY graduate now has his name atop the prestigious Rochester Institute of Technology's B. Thomas Golisano College of Computing and Information Sciences.

Rodeo, NM: John McAfee

The founder of McAfee Software, the largest anti-virus software company in the world, is currently co-founder and owner of an aerotrekking company called Sky Gypsies. He sold McAfee in 1999 and now spends his time flying air trikes— contraptions that look like motorcycles with wings, which allow you to soar mere feet above the ground over the painted canyons of New Mexico and Arizona. The software-engineer-turned-yoga-teacher-turned-desert-aerotrekker built a new town in New Mexico replete with its own coffee shop and movie theater to satiate his current passion. McAfee has created a new world for himself, eschewing the material world for more transformative experiences. He says in his New Age vernacular, "Be skeptical of the majority. Meet every event fresh, unencumbered by presuppositions. If we all walked the same road, there could be no discoveries, no mysteries, no new things. So make your own path." He is making his new path far from Silicon Valley where his multimillion-dollar fortune was created. In fact, he doesn't even use a computer much anymore. Don't e-mail him, just call him at the coffee shop in Rodeo.

Sacramento, CA: Marvin "Buzz" Oates

Founder and owner of the Buzz Oates Group of Companies, the largest commercial real estate and management company in Sacramento and the source of his billion-dollar fortune. His early aspiration was simply to own a shop that manufactured keys. A former fighter pilot, he accomplished his dream with the $2,000 he saved from his air force pay. His A&A Key Shop grew into a building supply company, which allowed him to begin building and owning commercial real estate. When he was in the seventh grade, the teacher asked all the kids that age-old question, "What do you want to be when you grow up?" His fellow students offered the usual professions: firefighter, police officer, doctor, lawyer. Oates blurted, "I want to make keys." The class erupted in laughter, but no one is laughing now.

Salt Lake City, UT: Jon Meade Huntsman Sr.

The founder of $10 billion Huntsman Corporation, a chemical conglomerate. A devout Mormon, Huntsman is Utah's most famous billionaire and also happens to be the father of Utah's current governor. His name rests proudly on the main building at the Wharton School of Business, the main arena at the University of Utah, and the law library at Brigham Young University. He is the author of *Winners Never Cheat: Everyday Values We Learned as Children (But May Have Forgotten)*. His passion currently is the Huntsman Cancer Institute at the University of Utah. He is not slowing down. Huntsman is building another business empire through his newly established $1.4 billion private equity group. He's also trying his hand at real estate development in the Grand Tetons of Idaho.

San Antonio, TX: Billy Joe "Red" McCombs

A natural-born salesman and businessman, McCombs left the University of Texas Law School to begin his career as a car salesman. Not content to work for the other guy, he soon became the sole owner of Red McCombs Automotive, which is today Texas's largest automobile group, selling Ford, GMC, Pontiac, Scion, and Toyota. He is co-founder of Clear Channel Communications, the entertainment conglomerate; owns McCombs Energy in Houston; and is a major commercial real estate owner and developer in Texas. He once owned the NBA's San Antonio Spurs and Denver Nuggets and the NFL's Minnesota Vikings before selling all three franchises for mucho profits. The University of Texas named its business school the McCombs School of Business.

San Diego, CA: Charles Brandes

Multibillionaire investment wizard and author of *Value Investing Today*, Brandes is a disciple of Benjamin Graham, the economist and professional investor who was the original proponent of the value investing principles that the world's richest man, Warren Buffett, and Brandes practice today. Brandes Investment Partners manages $95 billion and favors out-of-favor stocks that he believes have intrinsic value.

Sandpoint, ID: Dennis Pence

The co-founder and chairman of Coldwater Creek (NASDAQ:CWTR), the women's specialty apparel company. The retail and catalog empire was created by Pence and his former wife, Ann, in 1984 to give older women fashionable, yet affordable, choices in clothing. They launched the catalog-only line of women's accessories and a few Native American–inspired gifts with their $40,000 life savings. Although their marriage didn't last, the company has. Today Coldwater Creek has a market cap of half a billion dollars.

San Francisco, CA: Larry Page

The LEGO-loving co-founder of the Google juggernaut. This East Lansing, Michigan, native got his tech savvy genetically: His mother and father both taught computer programming at Michigan State University. His father later joined the faculty of the University of Michigan in Ann Arbor, where Larry received his undergraduate degree. It was in graduate school at Stanford University, however, that his life changed dramatically. He met his Google co-founder, Sergey Brin, and both went on to build the world's most powerful search engine.

Savannah, GA: Robert Jepson Jr.

The founder of the Jepson Corporation, which he created for the express purpose of buying undervalued, distressed companies. He successfully turned around nineteen companies and ultimately sold them all at handsome profits. "It was nineteen deals made in heaven," says Jepson. This success allowed the Jepson Corporation to become the fifth-fastest-growing public company in America in the 1980s. He says, "It was Shangri-la. We minted many millionaires." Shortly after the sale of the company, in 1989, he was lured out of early retirement to become the CEO and chairman of Kuhlman, an electric transformer company with a market cap of $70 million. He moved the Kuhlman headquarters to Savannah, diversified by buying competing market leaders, and turned the firm into a billion-dollar concern within six years before selling it to Borg Warner in 1999. The third leg of the wealth-creation stool was Tulsa, Oklahoma–based Coburn Optical Industries, maker of the machinery responsible for edging, polishing, and shaping eyeglass lenses. Jepson bought it all for debt and sold the company in 2000. Today he runs his family office and spreads his wealth generously, especially to the Jepson School of Leadership Studies at the University of Richmond.

Scottsdale, AZ: Bruce Halle

The founder and chairman of Discount Tires, a multibillion-dollar tire company that changes flat tires even if you bought them from someone else. From humble beginnings, the former marine first sold cars and insurance before finding his perfect pitch selling automobile tires. He started with one dilapidated store in Ann Arbor, Michigan, and today has more than seven hundred pristine stores in nineteen states. Virtually all of his executives started out in the company changing tires, just as he did. Halle's philosophy is, "Be fair, be truthful, work hard, be there on time, and help people." Helping people has helped Halle build one heck of a company, which he says is still the best reason to wake up in the morning—even more than forty years later. "There is nothing more fulfilling than owning your own business and seeing that business create jobs for good people and value for good customers."

Seattle, WA: William Gates III

Who doesn't know the third richest man in the world? Gates is still today the largest single shareholder of Microsoft, even though he is spending the majority of his time running the Bill and Melinda Gates Foundation—the largest foundation in the world. A middle child from a prosperous Seattle family, he nevertheless proved highly ambitious—ambitious enough to drop out of Harvard when he realized that Intel had manufactured a chip affordable enough to create the personal computer revolution, and that software would be the brains of all those computers.

Sioux City, SD: Denny Sanford

The majority owner of First Premier Bank and Premier Bankcard, which deals in subprime credit cards. The Minneapolis native located his company in Sioux City because of lenient anti-usury laws. He vows to die broke, spending most of his $3 billion fortune on philanthropy. Sanford has already given $400 million to create the Sanford Health Center, formerly known as Sioux Valley Hospitals and Health System, which he hopes will someday soon have the cachet of the Mayo Clinic. Sanford has tennis shoes that read WOLT—World's Oldest Living Teenager.

Spartanburg, SC: George Johnson

The former attorney, South Carolina legislator, South Carolina state development board chairman, South Carolina Chamber of Commerce president, and president of Blockbuster and Extended Stay America is one of the nation's busiest and most successful entrepreneurs. The oldest of three sons, Johnson graduated from Wofford College and received his law degree from the University of South Carolina. He began his entrepreneurial career in the grading business and graduated to the waste disposal business, a company that he sold to Wayne Huizenga of Waste Management. This was the beginning of a lifelong partnership. He joined Huizenga at Blockbuster and enjoyed one of the great entrepreneurial rides of all time. They eventually sold Blockbuster to Viacom for $8.4 billion. Johnson then developed the concept for the hotel chain Extended Stay America. Its first hotel opened in August 1995 in Spartanburg; the company went public in December 1995 and was sold to Blackstone for more than $3 billion. Johnson is chairman of Johnson Development Associates, which controls over four million square feet of industrial office and retail space in the Carolinas. He is chairman of Advance America Cash Advance Centers, which has more than seven hundred branches nationwide, and is managing general partner of American Storage Limited, a chain of twenty-six mini warehouses. Johnson is a director of Extended Stay America, AutoNation, Inc., Florida Panthers Holdings, Inc., Duke Energy Corporation, William Barnet and Son, Inc., and Morgan Corporation, Inc. He and partner Huizenga are now creating a new hotel company called OTO. There is nothing slow about Johnson other than his accent.

Spokane, WA: Harlan D. Douglass

The biggest real estate developer in his hometown, Douglass builds single- and multifamily homes, sits on the board of Northwest Bank, and invests in local companies such as Eagle Hardware and Garden.

St. Louis, MO: Jack Taylor

Chairman of Enterprise Rent-A-Car. The former World War II navy Hellcat fighter pilot served aboard the USS *Enterprise* before building what has become the largest car rental company in the country. He now owns National Car Rental and Alamo as well. Worth more than $14 billion, Taylor developed his love of cars as a salesman for a Cadillac dealership in St. Louis. He worked his way up to sales manager and convinced his boss to let him set up a car leasing business at the dealership. Taylor offered to take a 50 percent pay cut and put up $25,000 of his own money to own 25 percent of the leasing business. That business became Enterprise Rent-A-Car, one of the largest privately held companies in the country. The company today has over fifty-five hundred stores and still abides by Taylor's original philosophy: "Take care of your customers and employees first and profits will follow."

Syracuse, NY: Robert J. Congel

Founder of the Pyramid Companies, which he started in 1970 and still runs today. Congel claims that Pyramid is the largest privately owned developer of malls and entertainment complexes in America. Under his leadership, Pyramid built, owns, and manages sixteen shopping centers in New York and four in Massachusetts totaling more than 19.2 million square feet. According to the Pyramid Web site, Congel's company generates approximately $5 billion in annual sales.

Toledo, OH: Paul Ormond

Founder, chairman, and CEO of HCR Manor Care, Inc., the largest long-term care company in the United States, which was bought by the Carlyle Group (helmed by David Rubenstein, Washington, DC's RMIT) in late 2007 for $6.3 billion. This was a big payday for the CEO—who was already one of the highest paid in America. Ormond continues to lead the company he built after the leveraged buyout. HCR Manor Care has a network of more than five hundred nursing homes, assisted living facilities, outpatient rehabilitation clinics, hospice and home care agencies, and approximately sixty thousand employees. Ormond received his MBA from Stanford.

Trenton, NJ: Jon Corzine

Governor of New Jersey, he made his fortune on Wall Street when he served as the CEO of Goldman Sachs, one of the most prestigious investment banks in America. Now the richest self-made governor in history, with a fortune just under the half-billion-dollar mark, Corzine is a farm boy who grew up in Willey Station, Illinois. He is a Phi Beta Kappa graduate of the University of Illinois at Champagne-Urbana and received an MBA from the University of Chicago School of Business.

Tucson, AZ: Jim Click

This Oklahoma native moved to Tucson in 1971 and quickly made his mark, becoming one of the youngest automotive dealers in the country by age twenty-seven. Since then, he and his cousin Bob Tuttle have built up an impressive array of dealerships in Tucson and Orange County, California. They also purchased a controlling interest in Union Bank in 1978. It later became

Arizona Bank, before being purchased by Compass Bank, where Click continues to serve on the board of directors. He has lived by his father's creed, "Find something you truly love to do and retire for the rest of your life." Click may live in retirement land, but he is anything but retiring, and he never plans to stop working.

Tuscaloosa, AL: James I. Harrison Jr.

The patriarch of Alabama's first family of pharmacy in Tuscaloosa. Harrison began with one small mom-and-pop pharmacy (his parents') and turned Harco into one of the largest drugstore chains in the country before selling to Rite Aid in 1997. Harco, Inc., was founded in 1967, and Harrison ultimately built and operated 153 Harco Drug stores, fifty-five Carport Auto Parts stores, and seven Harco Totalcare (home health care) stores. The Harrison name sits atop the Auburn University School of Pharmacy. He says, "I'm the happiest guy on earth. I have a great family, I have had three great companies, and with my foundation work today, I'm doing something I love more than anything I have ever done in my life."

Washington, DC: David Rubenstein

Co-founder of the Carlyle Group, one of the largest private equity investment companies in the world, with more than $80 billion under management. From very modest circumstances in Baltimore, he raised himself to the top echelons of political power as a domestic policy adviser to President Jimmy Carter before creating his $3-plus-billion fortune buying and selling companies. Rubenstein, who raises the cash for Carlyle, is a lawyer by training, a salesman by practice. He seemingly sits on virtually every cultural board in America, from the Kennedy Center in Washington, DC, to Lincoln Center in New York. Rubenstein purchased the 710-year-old Magna Carta from Ross

Perot for $21.3 million (it now resides at the National Archives) and underwrote the discovery of an ancient Torah found buried in Auschwitz.

Wichita, KS: Phillip Ruffin

The billionaire best friend of Donald Trump made his fortune in casinos, convenience stores, real estate, and hand trucks. Ruffin is the owner of New Frontier Casino in Las Vegas, the Trump International Hotel and Tower, and several acres right on the Vegas Strip. He got his start in the convenience store business in 1959 without any financial partners and believes strongly that you don't get rich working for someone else. Ruffin does not believe in God; he believes in living life to the fullest, and he does.

Wilmington, DE: Charles Cawley

The co-founder of MBNA—Maryland Bank National Association, the pioneer of the affinity credit card marketing business now owned by Bank of America. The Georgetown graduate built MBNA alongside Alfred Lerner in the bowels of an abandoned supermarket and turned it into one of the fifty most profitable companies in America.

He first convinced his alma mater to sponsor a credit card for Georgetown alumni. This led to more than three thousand affinity groups following suit: universities, lawyers, doctors, nurses—you name it. He thought these affinity groups would keep users from searching for cards with lower interest rates. He was right. Along his success journey, he became a symbol of corporate excess, having earned over $50 million a year in salary and lavishly using corporate jets to entertain the Bush family and Washington heavies. He stepped down after a contentious board fight in 2004, according to the *New York Times*. Cawley racked up a huge fortune, though, with a simple philosophy of business and life: "Life by the inch is a cinch . . . life by the yard is hard."

Woodside, CA: Larry Ellison

This Bronx-born billionaire founded Software Development Labs, which ultimately became Oracle Software, the principal wealth-creation mechanism of his $25 billion net worth (he owns 20 percent of Oracle). Adopted by his aunt and uncle, Ellison was raised in Chicago. His best buddy is Apple's Steve Jobs. Thrice divorced, and famous for his spending habits, it's a wonder he is one of the richest people in America. He has all the billionaire toys: the yacht, the $200 million Japanese mansion complete with a reproduction seventeenth-century Kyoto teahouse. He has been cautioned by his financial advisers that even a billionaire needs a budget. Mike Wilson penned the story of his life, titled *The Difference Between God and Larry Ellison*. The not-so-subtle subtitle reads: *God Doesn't Think He's Larry Ellison*.

CONCLUSION

So what have I learned after my cross-country journey peeking into the fertile minds of America's RMITs? First, I have seen how generous the rich can be. They are generous with their time, generous with their thoughts, and, yes, generous with their money. On the other hand, they are not saints. They are not without their blemishes. You don't get to be mega-rich without ruffling a few feathers along the way. Creating great wealth can cause pain to others at times. When a private equity maven builds his wealth by chopping jobs, it causes pain for many. When an activist investor institutes a nasty proxy fight, it can make the lives of those running the company pure hell.

Perhaps the most astonishing thing I learned was that RMITs are genuinely happy—most of them anyway. They sought success first, and their wealth was simply the well-earned by-product, merely a barometer of their success. I have learned that they have an incredibly insightful sense of self; they have found their perfect pitch. They are independent in spirit—that's why they own and run their own companies. They are action addicts who rarely confuse activity with accomplishment, and they are obsessive about success, but in a good way, in most cases.

Their passion and energy for hard work are nearly insatiable, but to them work is not a job—it is a pleasure. They make things happen and enjoy the by-products of their accomplishments. Most are surprisingly humble, though extremely proud of their scorecard. They're proud because they have faced failure head-on and slain more than a few dragons with their dogged determination. They are nothing if not resilient in the wake of the inevitable storms and obstacles almost all of them encountered along their success paths.

RMITs don't remotely resemble the traditional "millionaire next door." First, they are way richer—with an average net worth of $3.5 billion, though that average number is skewed because of the superior fortunes of double-digit billionaire RMITs: Bill Gates (53b), Sheldon Adelson (26b), Larry Ellison (25b), Larry Page (19b), Sergey Brin (19b), Michael Dell (17b), Kirk Kerkorian (16b), and Carl Icahn (16b). The median net worth, however, is more representative—still a highly respectable $1 billion.

RMITs are also far different from the so-called millionaire next door because, while they live relatively quiet lives, in most cases their lifestyles are anything but austere or stoic. They enjoy their money and are not afraid to spend their hard-earned dollars. Three-quarters have a private jet—the lifestyle gift that is simply too hard to resist. There are more than thirty yachts. Some have cocooned themselves into a kind of isolation that seems lonely to an outsider peeking through their iron gates, but those are the rare few. The vast majority are making a difference in the town they most love and can't imagine living, working, or succeeding anywhere else. Seemingly instinctively, these American success stories have a masterful moral compass that has served them well and continues to guide them. There is not a felony conviction among them that I could uncover. And like the old Smith Barney advertisement: They made their money the old-fashioned way—they earned it.

As noted earlier, eighty-four of America's RMITs are college graduates, two are college dropouts, and fourteen didn't attend college at all. Ten went to Ivy League schools, seventy-six are married, sixty-four are still married to their first wife, fifty-two are Republicans, twenty-nine are Democrats, nineteen are independents, three give all the glory for their wealth to God, and two admit to being atheist. Thirty percent of RMITs are first-born, 15 percent second-born, and 12 percent are the babies of their families. A whopping eleven are the only child in their family.

I have seen firsthand that these American success stories are proudly persuasive and credit much of their success to their communication skills, but most of them acknowledge that doing what they love is the real key to their success and wealth. They surround themselves with the best and brightest people, recognizing wisely that they don't have all the answers, but are confident that they know where to get those often elusive answers and solutions. They are eternal students, constantly questing for that next level of learning and exploration. They have a voracious hunger for knowledge and absolutely no appetite for retirement.

That wise philosopher and comedian, Mae West, perhaps said it best: "I've been rich and I've been poor and believe me, rich is better!" Mae was right, but only if your gain is the result of some real value you have contributed to a worthwhile enterprise or from a significant difference you have made in your community. RMITs are rich in the richest sense of the word. Here's hoping you meet a similar fate.

ACKNOWLEDGMENTS

There were times as I was writing this book when I felt like I was living in solitary confinement. I wasn't the smartest person in the room, either—but I was the only person in the room—and there were times when I didn't particularly like that guy.

I want to thank all of the RMITs and RWITs for their time and insight into this project. They truly are generous in the richest meaning of the term. They were generous with their time certainly, but more important generous with their stories, their insights, their personal success formulas, and even their failures. If it sounds as though I really like these people, it should. As hard as I tried to be a totally dispassionate journalistic observer of these big bucks creators, I found that a very difficult, near impossible task. Yes, I admire what they have accomplished, I respect the way in which they have grown their wealth, and I appreciate their generosity of spirit. Some of these super-successes were initially disinclined to be interviewed because of their laudable humility. However, when they understood that they could make a real difference in the lives of so many just by sharing their unique and very personal experiences, most accepted my invitation with pleasure. We are all better for their generous decisions.

Fortunately for me, just as I was about to be sick of myself, there was always someone sliding sustenance under the door and offering me a much-needed helping hand and more than a word or two of encouragement. To those that I lovingly refer to as team

RMIT, I offer my appreciation and eternal gratitude. First, I thank the greatest support staff in the world—my wife, Connie, and our three sons, Cole, Chance, and Charles—for their unwavering love and belief in me. Thanks to Jane Berentson and John Koten, my colleagues at *Worth* magazine, who came to the rescue when I threw out the challenge to come up with a new and different way to view the wealthy in America for our tenth-anniversary issue. That special anniversary issue that we titled The Richest Person in Town was Jane's idea. It was the inspiration for my desire to dig deeper into the lives of America's greatest self-made success stories to determine what really makes them tick, and what lessons we could all learn from them. Alison Parks was my stalwart partner during the exciting and, at times, challenging *Worth* expedition—and I couldn't have asked for a smarter or more competent collaborator or better friend with whom to enjoy the ride. Patrick Sheehan edited my words at *Worth*, always making them more lyrical and my observations more trenchant; he was, of course, the first person I asked to read my manuscript. His insights and suggestions were, as usual, on the money. Christian Kunkel, my overqualified and underpaid RMIT intern, did so much of the initial spadework to find the most successful self-made person in each town that I am sure his hands are still throbbing from the digging. Susan Weaver, my producer, could run a Fortune 500 logistics company blindfolded. She arranged dozens of interviews, arm-wrestled too many RMIT assistants to count, and always kept the interview process running like a Japanese train. My agents Dan Ambrosio and David Vigliano shepherded me and the *Richest Man in Town* idea into the right hands at Grand Central Publishing with great skill. My attorney, Marc Chamlin, kept everyone on their toes and offered immeasurable insight and encouragement. I owe special thanks to my editor, Rick Wolff, for his belief in this project, his constant encouragement, and his gentle hand on my manuscript. I'm immensely grateful to all.

INDEX